The Black Experience in Maryland

By

VERA F. ROLLO

Second Edition, Revised

1984

MARYLAND HISTORICAL PRESS
9205 Tuckerman Street
Lanham, Maryland 20706

ACKNOWLEDGEMENTS

Every writer of history must seek out knowledgeable people to give the author insights and information. This writer would like to acknowledge her debt to the many people who assisted her in developing *The Black Experience in Maryland.*

Among those giving of their time and interest are: Dr. Benjamin Quarles, Department of History, Morgan State University; Baltimore City Public Schools; Dr. M. Sammy Miller, Chairman of the Department of History, Bowie State College; Dr. Martha Putney, formerly Chairman of the Bowie State College Department of History; Dr. Walter Fisher, Director of the Soper Library, Morgan State University; and to Mr. P. W. Filby, formerly Director of the Maryland Historical Society.

For their time and assistance, the author also wishes to thank Mrs. Elizabeth Murphy Moss, of the *Afro-American* newspaper chain, and Dr. Herbert M. Frisby, who offered much assistance in the chapter pertaining to the life of Matthew Henson.

Thanks are due, also, to those members of the U. S. Congress and the Maryland General Assembly who so kindly gave information on their experiences in Maryland. Justice J. Thurgood Marshall and his staff provided essential information on his work in the United States Supreme Court and on important decisions of that court.

When used together with other accounts of Maryland's past, this book, will help one to obtain a broader understanding of Maryland history.

The bulk of the research and writing of this book was done originally as a part of the work involved in writing the author's history of Maryland, *Your Maryland*, which was published in a revised, third edition in 1976. Portions of that book were extracted for this one and certain new text and illustration were added. This was done in order that *Black Experience in Maryland* might be used to supplement such histories of Maryland that lack its special insights and material.

Gratefully, the author acknowledges the assistance of many people who have helped her in her research and writing. Some of these are named in the Acknowledgments section.

It is the writer's hope that this story of the black citizens of Maryland will serve as a tribute to the Americans, men and women, black and white, who have worked so well to develop the State of Maryland.

Vera F. Rollo
Lanham, Maryland
1984

_____

Library of Congress Catalogue Card Number
79-64802
ISBN 0-917882-09-1

Printed in the United States of America.

CONTENTS

A LIST OF INTERESTING MARYLAND EVENTS

1500-1600	Explorers from Europe sail American waters.
1619	First Black persons are landed at the English colony of Jamestown, Virginia.
1628	A trading post is built on Kent Island by William Claiborne of Virginia.
1632	Cecil Calvert, second Lord Baltimore, is granted the Maryland Charter.
1634	Calvert's colonists, on the *Ark* and the *Dove*, arrive in Maryland waters. St. Mary's City is established.
1649	Maryland Assembly passes an "Act Concerning Religion."
1664-1692	Laws are passed in Maryland which reduce the rights of Black Marylanders.
1694	Maryland's capital is moved from St. Mary's City to Annapolis.
1729	Baltimore Town is established.
1776-1784	The American Revolution is fought.
1776	Maryland declares her independence of England and adopts the first State Constitution.
1783-1784	Annapolis is temporary capital of United States. While in Annapolis Congress ratifies the peace treaty ending the American Revolution.
1788	Maryland ratifies the Constitution of the United States.
1790	Reverend John Carroll is made first Roman Catholic Bishop in the United States.
1791	Maryland gives land to the United States for the District of Columbia.
1807	University of Maryland is chartered.
1808	U.S., following Britain's example, forbids international slave trade.
1810	Free Black men lose the right to vote in Maryland.
1811	Work begins on the National Road, extending west from Cumberland.
1812-1814	War of 1812 is fought between Britain and the United States.
1814	Battle of Baltimore takes place. "The Star-Spangled Banner" is written.
1825	Restrictions on voting and office-holding removed from Jews.
1828	The Baltimore and Ohio Railroad is begun in Baltimore.
1829	The Chesapeake and Delaware Canal is opened.
1831	Public and private funds given to help found state for free Black persons on the west coast of Africa, now Liberia, via Maryland State Colonization Society.
1844	World's first telegraph line built between Baltimore and Washington, D.C.
1845	United States Naval School (now Academy) established at Annapolis.
1850	C and O Canal, along Potomac, reaches Cumberland.
1859	John Brown launches his famous raid from a Maryland farmhouse.
1861	James Ryder Randall writes, "Maryland, My Maryland," now our State Song.
1861-1865	The Civil War rages. A main cause, dissent over slavery. In 1863 President Lincoln issues the Emancipation Proclamation.
1864	Maryland adopts the Constitution of 1864. This prohibits slavery officially.
1867	Maryland adopts the Constitution of 1867, our Constitution today, amended!
1867	President Andrew Johnson declares the Civil War officially over.
1870	Black men are given back the right to vote in Maryland.
1873	Johns Hopkins University established.
1892	*Afro-American* newspaper established.
1895	Baltimore builds first electric locomotive.
1906	Matthew Henson reaches N. Pole area with Peary.
1909	Aviation school begun at College Park.
1914-1918	The First World War is fought.
1920	Women are given the right to vote.
1920	Maryland coal mining reaches peak.
1941-1945	The Second World War is fought.
1952	Chesapeake Bay bridge is opened.
1954	Supreme Court ends segregation.
1957	Baltimore Tunnel is opened.
1965	Maryland-built satellite launched.
1969	Americans walk on the moon, aided by Goddard Space Flight Center, at Greenbelt, Maryland.
Future	Americans work together.

CHAPTER I

THE FIRST SETTLERS

Maryland Historical Society

The Ark and The Dove
— by Mall

Among the first settlers of Maryland were three men of African descent. Two of these pioneers, "John Price, a Negro, and Mathias Tousa, a mulatto," are mentioned as servants by the historian J. Thomas Scharf, in his *History of Maryland*, in describing the colonists' first settlement at St. Mary's City. These two men had probably been taken aboard when the *Ark* and the *Dove* stopped in the port at Barbados Island. Also, Father Andrew White, the Jesuit priest, in his narrative of the earliest days of the colony mentions that one of the four servants he brought into Maryland from Virginia in the year 1635 was Francisco, a "molato." We have the names, then, of at least three very early black immigrants to Maryland.

1

Plantation scene.
Library of Congress.

Black men and women had arrived in Virginia as early as 1619, brought to that colony as servants. In Maryland, as in most of the early English colonies, they came as slaves and servants. Likewise, persons of European descent came to the colonies as indentured servants. We must take note of the class system that existed in England, and to some extent, in English colonies in North America. Neither white nor black servants ordinarily expected to rise very far in the social order. A servant in those days usually was expected to remain a servant. Gradually, over the years, the free white man gained more social mobility, but about the best a black servant could hope for was to be able, sometimes, to earn his way out of bondage and perhaps obtain a little land of his own.

GATHERING FIRE-WOOD—A WINTER SCENE IN VIRGINIA.—[Sketched by W. L. Sheppard.]

In England in the same era, if a black person was a slave and was baptised as a Christian, he was then considered a free man. To keep black Christians from obtaining their freedom, and yet to be able to give them religious education, the Maryland Assembly passed a number of laws concerning blacks in 1664. These laws made slavery legal in Maryland. The laws said that black people might no longer work out their terms of indenture; and, if they already were bonded, then they must remain slaves for life. Another law was directed at marriages and children, where slaves were involved. Freeborn English servant women sometimes married black men, and these marriages previously had been recognized under the laws of England. The new rule in Maryland after 1664 declared that if a freeborn English woman married a black slave, she herself must serve that man's owner, and the children of that marriage would also be slaves owned by her husband's master! For those women already married to black men, the rule now was that the children must work for the master of the husband until they reached the age of thirty years. Clearly, these laws were made not only to discourage white women from marrying black men, but also to prevent, pretty generally, blacks from working out their terms of service with the hope of one day getting the same rights as indentured white servants.

In August of 1681, however, the Act of 1663-1664 was repealed. The new Maryland law declared that, thereafter, children born of white mothers and children born of free black mothers were to be free. Before 1692 more laws were enacted in Maryland to try to prevent and punish the practice of intermarriage between whites and blacks.

In Maryland other laws were later passed to prohibit English women from marrying black slave men, as well as to prohibit English men from marrying black women. As recently as 1966 and 1967 these colonial laws were enforced in Maryland, insofar as the making of a marriage between people of different racial backgrounds! Finally, the General Assembly looked into the matter and repealed the old law. As of July 1, 1970, marriage license office personnel in Maryland are no longer required to ask applicants for their racial background.

How They Came

The Royal African Company, formed by English businessmen and chartered by the King of England had a virtual monopoly on the legal slave trade to North America from 1672 to 1698. By the beginning of the eighteenth century (the 1700's) the import of black laborers was increasing, and independent traders were now sharing in the trade. Blacks had experience in farming in their African homeland and they knew how to grow crops and tend to farm livestock. Some blacks also had learned skills as artisans before they were brought to America. In America some of the blacks learned carpentry, metal working, shipbuilding, brickmaking and other construction and artisan trades.

Women in some cases learned to bake, weave, sew and nurse the young and the sick, here in America, increasing their original skills, and becoming valuable servants. Most black workers, both men and women, however, were employed in working the thousands of acres of land in the Maryland colony. To furnish this desirable labor, slave trading became one of the world's largest businesses and many fortunes were made in this cruel trade. In one year alone, 1698, Governor Francis Nicholson reported that 470 more blacks had been imported into Maryland.

The traders sought blacks, usually in Africa, to fill their ships. Blacks were often seized far inland and brought to the African coast by Arab traders, or by black chieftains who had captured them in some tribal warfare. Later, traders themselves were known to head expeditions to buy more blacks from villages many miles inland. The villages were normally visited in broad daylight, and the blacks for sale were purchased on the spot. But sometimes the traders would return again at night to seize and carry off the number of people needed to fill the slave ships.

Baltimore City, 1752.
Library of Congress.

The scenes on these ships engaged in the slave trade were apt to be terrible indeed. The captains were interested only in getting as many people onto the ship as could possibly make the trip, and in getting the slaves alive across the ocean to the markets in the Americas. The long ocean trip across the Atlantic was hard enough even in the best of conditions. But for the black captives it was likely to range from miserable to unbearable. There were many deaths due to crowding, disease, shock, and ill treatment. The captives were pushed into the dark holds of the ships, chained together and taken from all that was dear and familiar. It is little wonder then that there were many deaths, too, from despair and suicide. Records reveal as many as 300 to 500 persons were packed aboard some of the sailing ships used in the trade.

Thousands of blacks came to the Americas from a portion of the western coast of Africa known as the Gold Coast. This area is located on the southern side of the great bulge of the African continent projecting out into the Atlantic Ocean. Traders from the northern colonies, who were called Yankees, found the trade pretty well taken by Europeans on the Gold Coast. They were likely, then, to round the southern tip of Africa and set up bases on the island of Madagascar, just off Africa's southeastern coast. There African traders were waiting, with many blacks to sell.

Black Immigrants Enrich Their New Land

The unfortunate African, captured and sold into bondage, was able to bring little with him to America in the way of worldly possessions. Yet he did bring with him, if he were an adult, a certain amount of "cultural baggage." It was true that in being separated

5

from his own tribe and sent to America he was "uprooted" and lost much knowledge of African ways if he were only a young lad. Yet, a great deal of knowledge of farming, herding, irrigation and other farming skills was carried to America in the minds of these black pioneers.

Some of the Africans remembered, too, a good deal of their rich unwritten African literature—stories, legends, proverbs, riddles and ideas, passed down by word of mouth from father to son. The uprooted African did not always forget his old religious beliefs and his old customs. For that matter, the songs, dancing, new rhythms and ways of singing of the African were to greatly influence the development of a uniquely American music. The folklore of blacks from Africa became a part of American folklore. Later, the influence of African art was to be felt in both Europe and America.

Negro Pioneers

As the slave boys in Maryland grew up, some took care of the plantation or farm buildings and the livestock; others worked in the fields tending the food, forage, and tobacco crops. A few of the youngsters were brought to the great house of the master to learn to be butlers, valets, waiters and perhaps to learn skills of the artisans.

Some of the slave girls were trained to do household work. They were taught to be neat and polite and to be expert in cooking, cleaning, and in polishing silver and glassware. They might come to serve at the table or act as maids to the ladies of the household. They might help to keep the clothing and linens clean and pressed; or they might make clothing for members of the family of the master, or for the servants and farm workers. White girls were hired for low wages and taught these same skills.

Many black women were sent out to work in the fields. Some worked in the kitchens where food for workers was prepared. Women were also adept in the processing of the tobacco.

In towns blacks learned other skills and were more apt to be put to work in a home or a shop.

There was a sort of class system among the slaves themselves. House servants felt a bit above the artisan; but the artisan felt, in turn, a cut above the herdsman and coachman; and the fieldworker ranked lowest of all. Their clothing reflected this rank with the house servant clad in quite nice clothing and the poor field worker wearing very rough, plain clothing.

Much depended on the man who owned the slave and his family. He might be very kind, or he might be very cruel. In America blacks watched and learned. Some were fairly content, but most wished there was some way that they could be free.

CHAPTER II

BENJAMIN BANNEKER
AND THE ELLICOTT BROTHERS

DURING the American Revolution, John, Joseph, and Andrew Ellicott were kept busy, turning out wheat flour and corn meal at their mill on the Patapsco River. More and more grain came in to be ground. The Ellicott's first years had been greatly aided by Charles Carroll of Carrollton, who lived not far away. Their mill was the first in Maryland to produce flour and cornmeal, not at the rate of a few bushels a day, but in quantity. The Ellicotts put the production of meal and flour on a commercial scale.

Once the Revolution was over, the brothers knew that there would be a demand for flour, not only in the local area but with neighboring states and foreign countries, too. So they bought land at the corner of Pratt and Light Streets in Baltimore. There they built a warehouse and a wharf. Andrew's son, Elias Ellicott, was put in charge of the venture.

The Ellicott brothers found that to get their products to Baltimore and to help get grains to their mill, they needed a road. A road was built from the mill down to Baltimore. They later extended the road to the west, to Frederick. Gradually the little town that began with the Ellicotts' mill was to grow into today's Ellicott City, the county seat of Howard County.

The Inventive Ellicotts

Not only did the Ellicott brothers use their wits to build mills, equip them with machinery, and devise wharfs and roads, but as time went on, they also started many other activities in Maryland. For example, they opened a big general store near the mill which became a popular place for farmers and planters to shop and trade.

Of course, the children of the workers needed education. So the three young Quakers from Pennsylvania decided to establish schools. The Ellicotts had brought their families to Maryland from Pennsylvania as soon as they could. They built sturdy houses of stone. Construction continued without a pause as the brothers put up warehouses and other places of work, schools and homes.

Inventiveness enabled the Ellicotts to provide their mill community with a water supply system just as they also introduced, probably for the first time in Maryland, a way of irrigating fields. Mechanically-minded John Ellicott invented a brake for wagons, which helped control the heavy wagons on steep hills.

Among the buildings they constructed and equipped was a mill to grind chunks of plaster (lime) shipped from Nova Scotia, into powder. This, the Ellicotts demonstrated, could be used, along with other fertilizers and certain crop rotation, to turn worn-out tobacco land into producing land. The Ellicotts urged Maryland growers to turn to wheat growing, because it was a profitable crop which left the land productive.

Joseph Ellicott loved to make clocks. He is said to have invented the first four-sided clock made in this country. His son, Andrew, too, was scientifically inclined and very talented, as we shall see. Joseph, the son of the original Joseph who came to Maryland, devised and tried out, in 1789, a steam-propelled boat. The loss of his arm in testing the vessel prevented him from perfecting his design.[1]

Andrew Ellicott

The Ellicott family, following the American Revolution, took an active part in local, state, and national affairs. They even helped with the planning of government activities both on national and state levels.

Andrew Ellicott led a very interesting life. He was an engineer, a surveyor, and an inventor and was always very scientifically inclined. He was to carry out many fascinating projects.

In 1789 he surveyed the land between Pennsylvania and Lake Erie for the United States government. It was on this trip that he made the first accurate measurements of Niagara Falls and the Niagara River. In 1792, he was made Surveyor-General of the United States. He traveled far and wide, going south to survey the boundary between Florida (then a Spanish possession) and the United States. Later, he was sent to extend surveys westward from the Mason-Dixon Line into the Ohio country.

Andrew Ellicott and his friend Benjamin Banneker worked with Pierre L'Enfant surveying and planning the city of Washington, D.C. After Major L'Enfant was dismissed (he was a most temperamental gentleman and left in a temper, taking the nearly completed plans of the city with him), Andrew Ellicott was selected to finish the work.

First Rail Terminus

Many more interesting details about the Ellicott family cannot be told for lack of space, but just a few facts will show the part they had in the development of Maryland.

In 1809, fire destroyed the Ellicotts' mill and many of the log houses. The mill and homes were rebuilt almost immediately. By the year, 1825, the town at the mill had grown to a population of about 3,000 persons. When the Baltimore and Ohio Railroad was constructed to Ellicott's Mills in 1831, the thriving community became the nation's first rail terminus.

The Ellicott family kept ownership of the mills until 1837. In the little city today there are many houses and sites to remind one that the town has played an important part in Maryland's history.

Near Ellicott's Mills there lived a remarkable man, Benjamin Banneker. He was born in 1731, the son of Robert and Mary "Bannaky." His grandfather had been brought to Maryland from Africa, and was known as Bannka; later, Bannaky. Molly Walsh bought Bannka to help her clear land that she had claimed, near today's Ellicott City. She had been an English maid, an indentured servant sent to Maryland to work out seven years of bondage. Having finally finished her term of servitude, she needed help in making a farm. Bannaky and Molly Walsh after a while decided to marry and among their children was a girl called Mary. Mary Bannaky when she grew up, bought a black called Robert, from a slave ship. Mary and Robert later on were married and had several children, among them, Benjamin.

A portrait printed on the title page of Benjamin Banneker's 1795 almanac.

The farm came to be called Bannaky's Springs because there were abundant springs of good fresh water on the land. The family made a good living there. The Bannaky family cherished and guarded their status as free blacks, for all around them members of their race were working in bondage. With knowledge he had brought with him from Africa, Benjamin's grandfather led waters, by means of ditches and little dams, from the springs to irrigate his fields, and so even in dry seasons the Bannakys usually raised good crops of tobacco. Benjamin helped with the farm work. It seemed likely that he would be a farmer all his life.

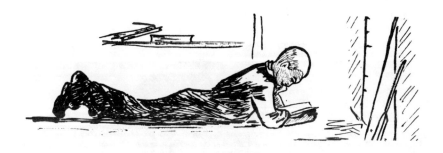

Using her Bible as a text, Benjamin's grandmother, Molly, taught the boy to read. In the summer of 1743, a Quaker schoolmaster, Peter Heinrich, came to the valley of the Patapsco River. Before long he opened a Quaker school for boys and he invited Benjamin to attend the school. It was there that the spelling of his name became "Banneker." Benjamin in due time became one of Peter Heinrich's most promising pupils. He was eager to get an education and worked hard on the farm and in the classroom. He learned to write and to do simple arithmetic.

When the Ellicott brothers arrived in the valley, they soon met the young Banneker and were impressed with his abilities. Soon he was helping to assemble the machinery of the mill. The Ellicott brothers talked with him, encouraged him, and loaned him books.

A turning point in his life occurred in Baltimore when Benjamin Banneker met a kindly man called Josef Levi. Seeing that Banneker was fascinated with his watch, Levi insisted on giving it to him.

Banneker took the watch home with him. In the months to come, he took the watch apart and learned how it worked. In the next three years he spent whatever time he could spare in working to make a clock. Most of the parts he carved from wood. He succeeded in his attempt and made what was possibly the very first striking clock made in Maryland. It ran faultlessly for many years, and many people came to see it. Banneker began to repair clocks and watches and to adjust sundials. He also worked on the very complex clock built by Joseph Ellicott.

Banneker and the Ellicott family were close friends. Books then were both scarce and expensive, but seeing that Banneker was sincere in his desire to learn, the Ellicotts loaned him many of their books on science. He put his amazing mind to work, learning advanced mathematics and other subjects in the field of mathematics and science. Banneker never married.

Benjamin Banneker

When his parents died, Banneker inherited the farm. To have opportunity to study his books, he devoted only enough time to working the farm to provide for his simplest needs. He became engrossed in the study of astronomy, and spent almost every good night scanning the sky for hours. He built a "work cabin" up on a hill. Inside he had a broad table and shelves for books. Latticed windows let in fresh air. Here he worked over intricate calculations. His fame in the area spread. Banneker's sisters lived nearby and they saw to it that he was left alone and made him comfortable.

This self-taught scientist made a complete and accurate "ephemeris" for the year 1792. An ephemeris is a calendar or an almanac, describing the locations of celestial bodies. His great knowledge of mathematics made this work possible. From 1792 until 1802 he published *Banneker's Almanac*. It was a very successful almanac, and his fame spread throughout the United States and in Europe.

On top of the work cabin on Banneker's land, there was now a window to allow him to study the skies through his telescope. For many years he worked, studied, and wrote there.

Almanacs had many uses in those days. Almanacs gave advice on farming, told when the moon would be full, when the tides would be high or low, and gave the reader an idea of what weather might be expected at certain seasons. If one's clock stopped on a frontier farm, one had only to consult the almanac to see what time the sun rose on a certain date, and then to reset the clock accurately by the sun. Also, for taking a boat trip, one consulted the almanac to find when the most favorable tides would occur.

The weather predictions Banneker included in his almanac were not just guesses. They were the sum of many years of study. Should an observer find for several years that the first two weeks of April were rainy in a certain locality, then he could put this prediction into an almanac. Essays, proverbs, jokes, and other items of interest made the almanac good reading.

At the same time that Banneker was calculating the future positions of the moon, sun, stars, and planets for his almanac, he was asked to help his friend Major Andrew Ellicott, and he agreed. Major Ellicott had been appointed the Chief Surveyor for the new capital city of the United States, Washington, D.C. He was responsible for gathering his own corps of draftsmen and assistants.

Ellicott and Banneker were soon working with Pierre L'Enfant, planning a city with a grid of streets, diagonally crossed by broad avenues. L'Enfant was a very talented man, but he was also not very easy to get along with. He liked to guard his plans and maps, so that selfish speculators would have no chance to buy up land for personal profit. L'Enfant intended to finish his plans, print hundreds of copies of his report, and then release it all over the country at an appointed moment so that everyone would have the same chance to buy property in Washington, D.C. Banneker, as one of Ellicott's surveyors, often worked closely with L'Enfant, to whom he was loyal and courteous as well as being modest, and capable.

But, suddenly L'Enfant was dismissed from the project and left in March, 1792, taking with him the precious plans for the city. An emergency meeting of the Capital City commission in charge of the project, as well as the surveyors and engineers, was called by Thomas

Jefferson, now the Secretary of State.

Major Andrew Ellicott attended the meeting with Benjamin Banneker. Working from memory, Major Ellicott and Benjamin Banneker redrew L'Enfant's plans. The work of the survey and planning of Washington, D.C. went on. Major Andrew Ellicott was now assigned the task of finishing the work begun by L'Enfant. You may be sure he relied upon his friend, the remarkable, sixty-one-year-old Benjamin Banneker.

Mural in the Maryland House, Aberdeen, Maryland, by William A. Smith. It shows Banneker and Major Ellicott in the field.

Courtesy Maryland Department of Highways.

Banneker adopted the Quaker style of dress. With the years his hair whitened. He is said to have looked very much like Benjamin Franklin, with the same features and the same set of the head. Physically, Banneker was tall and strong. He was very much loved and respected in the neighborhood of Ellicott's Mills.

On Sunday, October 25, 1806, he died. He had lived a long life in friendship and harmony with his fellow men. He had spent his years absorbed in many important interests, acquiring great knowledge, and doing the work he loved. His is a life of achievement to be remembered.

Banneker's farm location and burial ground is bounded by Oella Road and Cooper's Branch between Ellicott City and Catonsville.[2]

---

1 Celia M. Holland, **Ellicott City, Maryland, Mill Town, U.S.A.**

2 Silrio A. Bedini, **The Life of Benjamin Banneker**, 1972.

My hands! My dark hands! Break through the wall! Find my dream!
Langston Hughes

CHAPTER III

BONDAGE AND ITS PROBLEMS

To do all of the hundreds of tasks of the plantations, farms, towns, and homes, many workers were needed. Every free man, it seemed, wanted land for himself and wanted to work for himself; so labor was hard to get. For this reason, blacks were bought from slave traders by Maryland landowners. "Slavers" were the captains of ships sent out to buy workers in Africa or in the Caribbean from other traders.

What the Europeans were after—the labor of the captured black—was obtained. With this labor came much of the original progress of the English colonies. It was the work of strong, skilled, dark hands.

Colonial children often had to help with work.

From the earliest years of settlement, Maryland has benefitted from the efforts of black men and women, at work in Maryland homes and farming. There was much to be done in the new, wild land that was first colonized in the 17th century.

In America the African learned new customs and laws, a new religion and a new language, as well as how to do the many tasks awaiting him. Much of the agriculture of the country, especially in the South, depended on his labor. Slave rebellions were always expected and feared, but though often rumored, actually violence never occurred on a large scale. The white man was armed and there were strict laws, too well enforced to allow the slave to defy them. Then too, unfair as slavery was, the black servant often grew up believing that he owed loyalty to his owners. Many black servants loved their masters and kept them from harm by telling of planned uprisings.

The evidence of history tends to show that blacks in Maryland fared better than the people further south. Remember that from the beginning of their importation into Maryland, there were free blacks in the colony, and there continued to be many here. These people proved to be so important a part of the pool of workers that, in 1859, a convention of slaveholders refused to encourage the idea of passing a Maryland law to expel free blacks from the state. On the contrary, the convention recognized that these free workers were essential to business in the state.

It cannot be stated whether black people held in bondage in Maryland were treated with kindness or with cruelty; actually both sorts of treatment existed. Slavery, it should be recognized, was not good for either the slave or the master, for its psychological effects were bad for both. On the Eastern Shore plantation where Anna Ella Carroll grew up in the 1800's, the blacks appeared to be well treated. Yet, just a few miles away to the north, Frederick Douglass, born into slavery himself in this same period, saw many scenes of brutality and cruelty. He told of these events in his later writings and lectures in the mid 1800's.

Generally speaking, the blacks in the "border" states such as Maryland did have a better life than those held in bondage in the deep South. The Maryland plantation was generally operated by the family of the owner, while in the deep South there was much absentee ownership, with the plantation workers often left to the mercy of a merciless overseer. So, partly because of the laws restricting his actions and partly because of a better feeling between the races, there were very few incidents or uprisings in Maryland involving blacks. Slavery existed in the state for a little over two hundred years and yet the only serious uprising that apparently is recorded was an incident, thought to be spontaneous, in St. Mary's County, on April 7, 1817, when there were "several outbursts" involving about 200 slaves. No one was killed, though several people on both sides were injured, and two houses were sacked.

The great bulk of the importation of blacks occurred in the eighteenth century. Before that time immigration was fairly light. After 1800 the importation of laborers from Africa was discouraged by most of the governments of the world, including the United States, which after 1808 forbade international slave trade.

In Maryland it is especially true that black families have been here for a long time. As early as the year 1712 there were reportedly 8,000 blacks in Maryland and about 38,000 people of European descent. From that time the importation of African workers increased. They were brought in freely until 1780, when a heavy tax was imposed. Then, three years later, the importation of slaves from Africa was entirely forbidden by Maryland law.

From the beginnings of our national life in 1776*, probably the majority of the leaders hoped for a gradual ending of slavery in the United States. They realized that slavery was not in agreement with the ideal that all men were created equal and entitled to the free pursuit of happiness. With the invention of the cotton gin in 1794, by Eli Whitney, however, as noted before, it became profitable to grow cotton in the South and cotton fields seemed to demand slaves. So the national hope for gradual abolition faded.

---

* The American Revolution (1775-1783) set England's thirteen colonies free. These joined to form the United States of America.

Freeing enslaved people was no problem in those states having only a few people in bondage. But abolition was a problem in the Southern states where so much of the agriculture depended on having enough low-cost labor to work the great fields and where blacks made up a much higher percentage of the total population. So, slave-holders made excuses for keeping men and women in bondage. The slaveholder argued that the black was physically able to stand the Southern climate better than other workers; that he was better off learning the white man's ways and religion, and, after all "the Bible sanctioned slavery."

Anti-slavery forces succeeded in preventing the spread of slavery westward into the area north of the Ohio River, but the institution did spread south of the Ohio to the west, into Kentucky, Tennessee, Mississippi, and even onto the plains of Texas. With cotton becoming such a profitable crop, the price of good field hands moved sharply upward. This was especially true after the forbidding of more importation of slaves from abroad in 1808, though this law was certainly not always obeyed.

Within the United States the trading of slaves was still legal. Many people, even in the South, regarded the slave dealer with scorn and contempt, but this did not stop the business. One history[1] states that slave trading was the "cornerstone of the South's economy involving perhaps $150,000,000 in 1859-1860." In Maryland, where farms and plantations had more blacks in bondage than were needed, there was the temptation to sell away excess workers. It was realized that it was not morally right to break up long established homes and families. Where, as happened often, the slaveholder preferred to free his black workers, he still knew that they had little chance for successful lives in the hostile society of that period. Free blacks also ran the danger of being kidnapped by criminal gangs to be sold in the South.

Yet there were many people in Maryland who wanted an end to slavery. The Quakers or the Society of Friends, were perhaps most active in demanding aid to persons in bondage. As early as 1700, they were speaking out against the evil and were insisting that all Quakers free their servants. In 1784 the newly-formed American Methodist Church, with a large membership in Maryland, spoke out against slavery. As a result, many wills were written containing instructions to free slaves, and, by 1860 due to all these influences, the state had almost as many free black people (84,000) as it had slaves (87,000). Maryland had at this time fewer slaveholders and slaves than any other Southern state.

Maryland in Liberia, **an oil painting by John H.B. Latrobe (1803-91).**
Maryland Historical Society

The Maryland Branch of
The American Colonization Society

The American Colonization Society was established in 1816 to relocate blacks who had been freed in the United States. Colonies were planned for the west coast of Africa in that area known as Liberia. This program found strong support in Maryland. Around 1831, both private and state funds were given to aid the colonization project. The colony of Monrovia was begun; and later, down the coast about two hundred miles another, known as the Maryland colony. These two colonies were later combined and the nation of Liberia developed from these activities. In that nation today there is still a part called "Maryland."

An interesting sidelight to the story of Maryland's part in trying to aid freed blacks, is the story of Dr. Samuel Ford McGill[2]. This young black was the son of an early Monrovian colonist. Since white physicians could not seem to survive the climate and diseases of that part of Africa, the Maryland State Colonization Society decided to train an acclimated black to fill the position, for the colony needed a doctor. Samuel McGill volunteered to undergo medical training though he knew that he would face obstacles and discrimination in any medical school he might enroll in. This was especially true if he were enrolled in a southern school. On the other hand, the Maryland sponsors were reluctant to let him study in the northern United States where he would be in contact with abolitionists and northern ideas of resistance to the whole institution of slavery.

Sure enough, McGill was not able to attend a medical school in Baltimore for very long, in 1836, before his classmates refused to let him go on. His sponsors sent him north to study under a physician in Vermont and later he studied at Dartmouth College. He was an outstanding student, even mastering the study of Latin by means of much self-directed effort. By 1840, Dr. McGill was the colonial physician of the Maryland colony in Liberia and held that post for many years. He was to do other important work there as well.

But colonization was not to be the answer to the problem of what was to happen to the freed slave. American blacks did not like the idea of leaving the United States and not enough volunteered to go to Liberia to make much difference in conditions here. So, though over $300,000 was spent over a period of twenty years, only about 1500 American black colonists were ever actually settled in Liberia.

There is an odd ending to this story. In 1931, the League of Nations investigated reports of slavery and forced labor being inflicted on the native Africans by the Americo-Liberians. The reports were found to be true. Steps taken to abolish the practice of slavery in Liberia were successful by 1936 and today, the nation is one of the world's most promising African republics.

Laws Affecting the Status of Black Persons in Maryland

Mention has been made of the colonial laws designed to prevent whites and blacks from marrying one another. There were other measures passed both in colonial days and later in the early days of statehood. These were designed to help slaveholders capture runaway workers, to prevent the free movement of blacks in bondage, and to prevent them from owning and inheriting property. All of these laws restricted the freedom of action of the slave.

Free families arriving in Baltimore, 1800's.
Leslie's, Sept. 30, 1865.

Drawing of a Plantation.

Free persons of African descent in Maryland found life very difficult for there were many laws to hamper them, too. All too often, free blacks were kidnapped and sold into slavery again. Then too, they were abused in business, had property damaged, and generally were harassed at every turn. Even so, the Maryland black progressed, letting his determination and hard work speak for him. Schools were set up in the early 1800's in Baltimore for adult free blacks and later, for a few of the black boys. A Catholic organization also started a school to educate black girls.

1 Frederic Bancroft, **Slave Trading in the Old South**.

2 Acknowledgement is made of the article by Penelope Campbell, "Medical Education for an African Colonist," published in the **Maryland Historical Magazine**, Vol. 65, No. 2, 1970.

We will not be satisfied until justice rolls down like waters and righteousness like a mighty stream.

Martin Luther King

CHAPTER IV

JOHN BROWN'S RAID

NOT far from Harper's Ferry, Virginia, on the Maryland side of the Potomac River, about two dozen children settled down to study. If they had trouble keeping their eyes open, it was not surprising. This Monday morning, October 17, 1859, was one of those gloomy fall days. The clouds pressed down on the mountains. There was a raw edge to the wind. The schoolmaster muffled a yawn himself at the thought of a long, quiet day ahead, full of readin', writin', and 'rithmetic.

The occupants of the schoolhouse could not know that they were living a day to be studied by many future students. As yet, no one in the school knew that John Brown, his two sons, and twenty men had slipped down out of the Maryland hills the night before. Armed with guns and Bowie knives, they had come, under the cover of fog, to the covered bridge that led to the town of Harper's Ferry.[1] The men had cut telegraph wires and captured the bridge watchmen.

On the Virginia side of the river, they had turned out the lights on the bridge and in the town. Moving swiftly in the dark, they had overcome the armory gate watchmen. Next, they took the buildings and the United States arsenal[2] itself. Not a shot was fired and the town had slept on, unaware that John Brown and his raiders had seized the arsenal!

Brown was a tall man, about sixty years old. Though his shoulders were slightly bowed, his figure was wiry and strong. Long, rough, white hair and a full beard surrounded "the face of a hawk." His burning eyes revealed the excitement of this moment. He, John Brown, was now ready to head up armies of blacks and sympathizers and force the South to free every slave. He felt sure that the slaves would rush to follow him. He was fanatical about this, and so strange, in fact, were his actions, that it seems doubtful that John Brown was entirely sane.

Back in Kansas a territory from which he had recently fled, he was wanted for murdering five men in cold blood. He was charged, too, with kidnapping slaves and smuggling them to freedom. For some months he had been a fugitive in hiding, but now he felt his moment had come. With all of the rifles and plenty of ammunition from the captured arsenal, he planned to lead the slaves to form a new nation. Since early July, he had been plotting his course and it felt good to go into action. His first objective was to capture the arsenal, and now that that step had been successfully taken, he felt sure hundreds of slaves would now rise up and join him at Harper's Ferry.

Back at the school house, the pupils and their schoolmaster knew nothing of all this. Their first inkling of trouble was the sound of horses and men outside, the jangle of trace chains and the screeching of slowing wheels as brakes were applied. The children's eyes grew round with fright when several men came in the door carrying pikes and guns. In no time, it seemed, the schoolhouse was full of big, wild-looking men carrying in boxes of ammunition and guns. The schoolmaster, recovering somewhat from his first surprise, and thinking of his children, asked if he might send them on home. The man giving orders objected, but the schoolmaster persisted and finally convinced the intruders that it was all right to let the children go. No one would believe their story at any rate until it was too late. The schoolmaster, they kept with them as a hostage.

Over on the Virginia side of the Potomac, about two miles from the schoolhouse, things were beginning to go wrong for John Brown. Workers were coming to work at the arsenal. One by one these men were captured and quietly herded inside and guarded. But rumors were beginning to fly through the town. Some people fled from Harper's Ferry, hearing that a whole army of anti-slavery men were taking over. A few began to hunt for guns and to think about organizing and defending themselves.

More news was on its way out of town. John Brown had finally let a train leave Harper's Ferry at 6:30 in the morning, after he had kept it there for five hours. Even so, when the train stopped an hour later at Monocacy Junction, the conductor, A. J. Phelps, could get no one to believe his story. For two hours, he continued to wire the railroad headquarters in Baltimore, before he at last convinced the outside world that something strange was going on at Harper's Ferry. The B & O officials then notified the War Department in Washington.

About this time, too, messengers had reached nearby Charles Town, then a part of Virginia. The militia unit there was ordered out and soon was marching to Harper's Ferry, its members armed with every sort of old gun and sword imaginable. The militia surrounded the abolitionist-held arsenal grounds and waited for more help to arrive.

Brown's men holding the schoolhouse soon learned that Brown himself and the others at the arsenal were surrounded and outnumbered. No aid had come from slaves or northern anti-slavery sympathizers and hopes for an uprising were evaporating. The raiders at the schoolhouse concluded that the best thing for them to do was to save themselves. So, much to the schoolmaster's relief, they left.

Meanwhile, down in Harper's Ferry, the noose was tightening for John Brown and his men in the arsenal. At first, full of confidence, he ordered his men to hold out saying that soon slaves and anti-slavery sympathizers would be there to help. But early on the morning of Tuesday, October 18, a company of U.S. Marines commanded by Colonel Robert E. Lee, captured John Brown and his men after a brief but bloody fight.

The strange happenings, however, were not entirely ended. The school children had, by this time, told their parents. One father, a farmer, hearing of the events at Harper's Ferry, decided there might be some connection to all that was going on. So, he hitched up a horse and went to Colonel Robert E. Lee.

Lee acted quickly in hopes of capturing the other raiders, and promptly sent a part of his company to the schoolhouse. The place was quiet and the raiders were gone; yet, proof of the truth of the schoolboy's tale was in the grim presence of two hundred carbines, two hundred revolvers, two hundred fifty pounds of gunpowder and quantities of cartridges, all stacked in the schoolhouse!

By the end of that Tuesday, five citizens of the town and a Marine lay dead, and nine citizens and another Marine had been wounded. As for John Brown's abolitionists, ten were dead and five of those taken prisoner had been wounded.

The next week, on October 25, 1859, John Brown and his men were brought to trial at Charles Town, Virginia. It was an odd trial. Brown lay on a cot in the court room part of the time. He was suffering from fatigue, ill health, and a poor memory, he said. Yet, he would not let his attorney reveal to the court that there was a history of insanity in his mother's family. John Brown told the court only that he wanted to free the slaves and take them to Canada.

The jury sat through all the strange speeches and heard the evidence for both sides. Then they left the court room and for half an hour the courtroom buzzed with low conversations. Finally, the door opened and the jury returned to the courtroom and took their places. The verdict was, "Guilty."

John Brown and six of his band (another had been found) were hanged. His name spread far and wide after this. Songs and poems were written about the Harper's Ferry raid. Anti-slavery people thought him a hero. Southerners, always worried about the possibility of a slave uprising, were very bitter about him. The news, the gossip, and the bitter feelings that John Brown's raid had roused added to the ever more difficult problem facing a nation, part of which was for slavery, and part against it.

The guns were removed from the little schoolhouse. When the schoolmaster again faced his students, they could talk about the exciting events of the past days, and they could ask whether this was just one raid, or whether it would be followed by others. Would there be peace, or was it possible that men would fight about this slavery question? Even the children on that Maryland hill overlooking Harper's Ferry could not help but wonder if there would be more fighting and violence over slavery; but they could not then realize that the story of the events they had experienced would be of historical interest to pupils like themselves in years to come.

---

1 Harper's Ferry was then in the state of Virginia. Later, the area became a part of a new state, West Virginia.

2 An arsenal is a place where guns and military equipment are made or stored.

A photograph and a portrait of John Brown.

CHAPTER V

FREEDOM

Freedom is and always has been America's root concern, a concern that found dramatic expression in the abolitionist movement.
                                                            Benjamin Quarles

More and more people in the year 1862 were urging President Lincoln to free the slaves. Lincoln had hoped to first make some definite plan for their future. Miss Carroll[1] had freed her own slaves some time before, but only after training them to make a living and finding work for them. She did not think, as some people did, that bands of free blacks would roam the city and country, robbing and killing. She did remember, however, their poverty and fears when freed in Maryland with no home and no way of earning a living. So she advised President Lincoln to plan for the future of black Americans and this he agreed to do.

Lincoln, in a conference on May 12, 1862, with seven congressmen, pointed out that it was no kindness to release blacks into communities where they would not be welcome and where they might not get land of their own. He believed that land might be secured for them if a colony were to be started in Central America, possibly in the area that is now Panama. He showed the congressmen a box of food and trade products, including mahogany, coffee, coconuts, and bananas, which he said were, "from Miss Carroll." Then Lincoln added, "This Anna Ella Carroll is the top of the Carroll race. When the history of this war is written, she will stand a good bit taller than ever old Charles Carroll did."

During the summer of 1862, Lincoln asked Anna to write out a paper explaining carefully the Central American relocation project. But, the pressure of events forced the President to move more swiftly than he wished in the matter of freeing blacks. By August 25, the capital city of Washington was in danger of capture by the

---

1 Anna Ella Carroll, was a Maryland lady. She was an author and one of Lincoln's military advisors. Her valuable work was little known until the 1930's.

The Civil War broke out in 1861 and lasted into the year 1865. Thousands of men died and thousands were hurt. Both Union and Confederate forces suffered terrible losses. When the war was over, the Union of the United States was still intact, slavery was gone from the land, the South lay devastated, its political and economic power crushed. Many years were to pass before the impact of the Civil War was to fade from the minds of Americans. Many years were to pass, too, before Americans of African descent were to have true freedom. Only today is that dream coming true.

The map, sketched below, shows the strategic position of the "border state" of Maryland, during the Civil War.

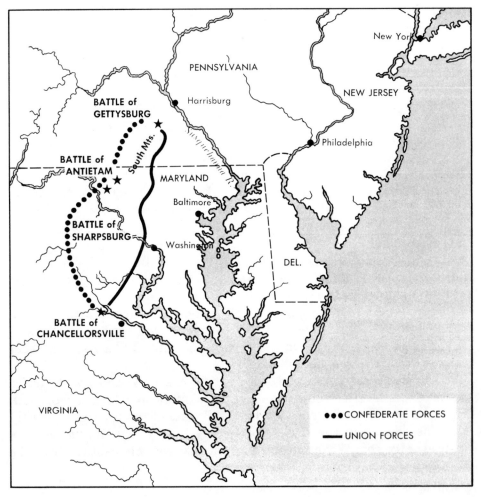

LEE'S OFFENSIVES, 1862–1863

An anti-slavery meeting on the Boston Common.
Gleason's, May 3, 1851.

Confederate army. Plans were made for the evacuation of the capital if necessary! Lee advanced into Maryland on September 3 and tried very hard to make the state a Confederate stronghold. It was then that Lincoln promised that, if the Confederates were pushed back across the Potomac, he would issue an executive order to free the persons held in bondage in the rebelling states of the South.

The Year 1863

"I, Abraham Lincoln . . . as of January 1, 1863 . . . all persons held as slaves within any state . . . now in rebellion . . . shall be then forever free." President Lincoln's proclamation was an Executive Order which freed thousands of black workers in those states which had seceded from the Union. Oddly enough, in some Union states this left the practice of slavery still technically legal. In Maryland, slavery did not become officially outlawed until November 1, 1864.

At first this seemed a wonderful day for black men and women. But though they rejoiced to be free, at last, still the abrupt end of their servitude left them with serious problems. They were completely unprepared for freedom. They were freed without jobs, homes, or plans for their future. They needed many things very quickly—such as education, jobs, and housing. However, each year thereafter saw black citizens making some gains, and learning and progressing, despite many obstacles.

A Union soldier.   **A Virginia cavalryman.**

1865: The Civil War Ends

The "War Between the States" was now about ended. In Virginia, Petersburg had eventually fallen and also Richmond. Lee at long last surrendered to Grant at Appomatox Court House, Virginia, on April 9, 1865. The South was shattered—its business wrecked; its plantations burned and deserted; railway lines torn up and the cities in shambles. Thousands of families mourned for soldiers who would never return home. Thousands more did come home, though often wounded and sick. Prisoners, too, were released. The treatment of these, by both sides had been disgraceful. They had been allowed to starve and suffer from cold and disease, in places filled with vermin and filth.

But all Americans were now free, and the United States was no longer a divided country—at least in the political sense of the word. The Civil War had been a cruel and costly one for both the North and South. Dazed, our nation was yet grateful that it was over.

Lincoln's plans for the peaceful rejoining of the Southern states to the Union, and his plans for helping black Americans get a new start, were not to be carried out. Relocation of black Americans would probably have been as unsuccessful as other colonization plans. Lincoln's leadership, however, might have helped blacks to move forward politically and economically more quickly than actually happened. On April 14, 1865, Lincoln was shot by John Wilkes Booth and died the following day.

The state of Maryland was in the odd position of having remained a part of the Union, which meant furnishing men and materials to the support of the North, while at the same time many people in the southern counties sympathized with the Confederacy and tried to help it. Due to this leaning toward the South, Maryland shared in the years after the War, in much of the oppression dealt out to the defeated Confederate states! Maryland was ruled by the military throughout the War and it was, in fact, not until January 31, 1866 that the Federal military rule was finally withdrawn. Then only was civil government returned to Maryland.

In the midst of the War, the Maryland Constitution in 1864 was rewritten. It reflected only the feelings of the men then in power in Maryland, the Unionists. The Constitution called for a strong oath of loyalty to the United States by every State official. Men who would not take this oath, because they sympathized with the Southern states, could not hold office in Maryland. According to the *Baltimore Sun*, three-fourths of Maryland's voters were not allowed to vote, due to the strict and searching loyalty tests at election time in the years following the adoption of the Constitution of 1864.

This feature among several others made the Constitution of 1864 very unpopular with the people of Maryland and in 1867, as soon as Maryland had regained control of her own affairs, another Constitution of Maryland was drafted and then ratified. It is the Constitution under which Maryland is governed today, though it has, of course, been amended many times.

The unpopular Constitution of 1864 had good features such as the abolition of slavery in Maryland, for example. This clause was retained in the next Constitution. Also, the 1864 Constitution provided for a uniform state system of education in Maryland. It also gave the state a Lieutenant-Governor and brought back the office of Attorney General. Since the man holding the post of Lieutenant-Governor was not popular in 1867, that post was abolished in the Constitution of 1867. In the 1867 Constitution, the hated loyalty oath was softened. The writers reached back to the Constitution of 1776 for their Declaration of Rights. It was a conservative Constitution.

It was April 2, 1867 when President Andrew Johnson declared the rebellion officially over, and this was two years after General Lee's surrender at Appomattox. These years might have been quite different if John Wilkes Booth had not succeeded in murdering President Lincoln.

Yet, despite the battles, the bitterness, and the postwar injustices, this new Union of America somehow held together. Never again was our nation to be divided so violently. The effects of the Civil War and the Reconstruction period that followed, however, were to last many years after the guns were silenced.

HARRIET TUBMAN (1815-1913) escaped from an Eastern Shore plantation when she was **twenty-five**. She led over three hundred Negroes to freedom. During the Civil War she served as a nurse and as a secret Union agent. She later helped many black people to obtain schooling and was, to the day of her death, always ready to extend a helping hand to people in need. This powerful sculpture was done by Frederic J. Thalinger.

Photograph, 1947, courtesy the Library of Congress.

CHAPTER VI

MARYLAND'S CITIZENS

We are Americans and as Americans we would speak to America.
Frederick Douglass

To exist is to change, to change is to mature, to mature is to go on creating oneself endlessly.

Henri Bergson

With the Civil War raging, on September 22, 1862, President Abraham Lincoln issued the famous Emancipation Proclamation. This was just after the costly Union "victory" at Antietam. Effective January 1, 1863, Lincoln's proclamation, as we have noted, freed all blacks enslaved in the states rebelling against the government of the United States. The proclamation of course did not free persons held in bondage in Maryland, because it was not a secession state. Not until November 1, 1864, was slavery actually ended in Maryland with the adoption of the State's new constitution. This Constitution of 1864 in addition to prohibiting slavery stated that persons supporting the Confederacy were to be barred from the right to vote and to hold public office.

Two years later, the Fourteenth Amendment to the Constitution of the United States (the Civil Rights Act of 1866) gave freed men the rights of citizenship. The amendment stated that no state should deprive any person of life, liberty, or property without the due process of law. The next amendment to the Constitution, the Fifteenth Amendment, gave the blacks the right to vote. This was reflected by Maryland law in 1870, when Black men were given the right to vote. Interestingly enough, up until 1810 in Maryland, free Black men had had the right to vote.

In a recent study of the black in Maryland politics[1] the research showed that since black men regained the vote in 1870, he has used it responsibly. Usually the Maryland black has voted with the Republican party and has helped sustain the two-party system in our state. In the early part of the twentieth century (early 1900's) blacks in Maryland prevented the loss of the voting privilege for the black

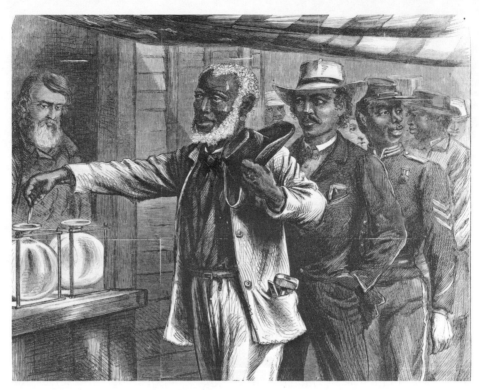

"The First Vote." Drawn by A.R. Waud.
Harpers Weekly, Nov. 16, 1867.

voter by using their political power. In the years covered by the Callcott study (1870-1912) it was found that few blacks were voted into office in Maryland. Today, the political recognition in Maryland that the black citizen has worked so long to achieve will soon be his.

In other Southern states, black voters were held back by both legal and illegal methods. In Maryland, however, open terrorist tactics seemed not to have been as popular as in the deep South. It cannot be said that there were not some illegal activities by terrorists, but such frankly secret groups such as the Klu Klux Klan seem not to have been widespread in Maryland. There was prejudice, to be sure, but at least the appearance of legality was maintained. The black Marylander had won respect and affection.

Coming up to modern times, still another important ruling was to affect citizens of African descent in Maryland, and elsewhere in the United States. It was the ruling made May 17, 1954, that the segregation of races was illegal in the United States.

After the Civil War

After the Civil War the people in the United States who had been held in bondage were suddenly faced with the problem of earning a living; and most of them did not have the land, the tools, the capital, or the training to do so. They were faced, too, with the problem of earning a place in a society hostile to them and one which was unwilling to give them their full rights of citizenship.

Blacks, who had always been denied equal educational opportunities, began immediately to seek schooling. People sympathetic to their hopes sent money and teachers into the South. Schools and colleges were started. There was by no means equality of opportunity as yet, but black leaders came forward to help with educational projects, and funds and volunteers were gathered by sympathetic white citizens.

But, toward the end of the nineteenth century, and in the early 1900's, laws were passed in many states that forced white and black people to live, work, study, travel and play separately, a condition that continued down to the present generation.

Black Men in American Military Services

During the American Revolution many black men accepted the British offer of freedom in exchange for service against the rebelling American colonists. The war offered for them the possibility of freedom if the British should win. On the other hand, the American Continental Army appeared not to want blacks to enlist, on the theory that they would not be able to become disciplined soldiers. Yet,

"Steuben at Valley Forge." Painting by Edwin A. Abbey, hangs in the Pennsylvania House of Representatives. It shows Baron von Steuben instructing American troops during the winter of 1777-1778.

Pennsylvania Dept. of Commerce

Academy Color Guard.

gradually this attitude changed, and in January 1776, General George Washington agreed to accept free blacks into the Continental Army. By 1778 the Second Maryland Brigade, for example, had sixty blacks in its ranks. In 1780 a Maryland law was an indirect admission that black men made good soldiers, for it made free blacks liable to being drafted into the State militia. It also allowed the recruitment of blacks still in bondage with the consent of the slaveholder.

During the Civil War, black men served on both sides of the conflict. In the South black men often built defenses, raised food, and provided much valuable labor. As Union forces entered the South, however, a large number of blacks flocked to the Union commanders and offered their services in return for their freedom. There were varying policies concerning this kind of help; yet it is true that many blacks indeed were helped to freedom in this way. They, in turn, helped Union forces with their work. In later stages of the war, black men served in the Union services both as soldiers and sailors. Some writers suggest that there were many such blacks in uniform, and that they practically won the Civil War for the Union. This of course is an exaggeration. Still, it is true that before the end of the Civil War, commanders on numerous occasions commended their black servicemen for their ability and for their courage.

Both World War I and World War II saw black men serving their country with courage and honor in the armed forces. Again, in the Korean War, and in the Vietnam War, the black soldier, sailor, and airman performed bravely.

Negro leadership in antebellum America was predominently ministerial, colored men in other professions being in short supply.

Benjamin Quarles

CHAPTER VII

RELIGION IN MARYLAND
A Comparison of Maryland Religions

ONE may wonder why people attend so many different churches. One wonders why should we not all attend the same church and worship in the same way. The reason seems to be that people hold differing beliefs. Also, people have different ways of worshiping their God and different ways of admitting new members into their church or temple.

Even so, all churches in Maryland share certain ideas. All churches, for instance, worship a Supreme Being, a God. Again, all want their members to be good people who are honest, brave, loyal to their religious beliefs and helpful to people in need. Churches and temples generally give advice and help to individuals, as well as helping the needy and working for special programs to aid people in general. Most churches help support orphanages and homes for the aged and the ill. Many Maryland churches build and support hospitals and help to support medical training schools. Most churches send medical aid and missionaries to other lands. Those people needing help, churches want to hear about, and they will gladly do what they can to help.

This remarkable fact of life is often ignored but it is very real. Religions have had a great deal to do with shaping our history, in Maryland, in our nation, and in our world. Since churches are important to history, in a *very* general way we will describe the churches that have been, or are, in Maryland.

Certainly one of the oldest religions represented in the state and nation is that of Judaism. It is also called the Hebrew religion. People sharing these religious views are also known as Jews. The history of the Hebrew people and their religion goes back 4000 years! It is the parent religion to most Maryland religions, for in our state the majority of our citizens belong either to Hebrew or Christian congregations.

Christianity branched off from the Hebrew religion almost 2000 years ago. The Hebrew people believe in one diety and have a very complex and strict code of behavior. They refer to their places of worship and study as temples or synagogues. Generally, the Jews prefer to reserve Saturday as their day of rest, study and worship. The basic holy books of the Hebrew people are the Old Testament of the Bible and the *Talmud*.

Christianity as a religion began almost 2000 years ago and is based on the teachings of Jesus. The holy book of the Christian churches is the *Holy Bible*, which is made up of the Old Testament and the New Testament. Christians share many beliefs and ideas in common with the parent religion, Judaism, but they vary on a number of points, too.

The Catholic Church used to be the only Christian church. In the year 1054 A.D., there was a split and the first Christian church found itself divided into the Roman Catholic Church and the Orthodox Church.[1] The Roman Catholic Church is the one that most Maryland Catholics attend. This church is headed by the Pope in Rome, Italy. The Christian churches, except for the Seventh Day Adventist Church and a few other denominations, have chosen to use Sunday for their day of rest and worship.

In the sixteenth century there was a move to resist the authority of the Roman Catholic Church — a movement known as the Reformation. Martin Luther was one of the first men to voice openly this protest against the authority of Rome. New Christian groups, like Luther's own Lutheran congregation, formed. These came to be called Protestant churches. Protestants, to be sure, share many beliefs of the parent church, the Roman Catholic Church. Members of Protestant churches, too, believe in Jesus and his teachings, and regard the *Holy Bible* as their basic religious book.

One of the Protestant religious groups that found a home in Maryland was the Society of Friends, whose members are often called Quakers. It is a religious group which advocates peace and whose members like very plain religious meetings without specially trained priests or clergymen. The Presbyterian church, another popular Christian denomination in Maryland, favors a more elaborate program of worship services and bases its teachings on Biblical doctrines. It is a conservative church. The Protestant Episcopal Church perhaps shares more things in common with the Catholic churches and is also quite a conservative church. It was formerly the Anglican Church, or the Church of England. Puritans were yet another group who came to Maryland quite early in the history of the colony. Puritans were very strict with themselves and rather intolerant of other religious groups. Puritanism, as such, died away in Maryland. The Baptist Church got its name from its practice of baptising its members, that is by totally immersing new members in water. It is a very active church and is very popular in many parts of the South. The Lutheran Church arrived in Maryland with the arrival of the German-speaking peoples, and another Protestant denomination, the Moravian Church, too, came here with German immigrants who settled in the Piedmont section of

Maryland. The United Methodist Churches have grown from early beginnings in Maryland and their members feel that each Methodist is a disciple of Jesus.

As you can see, the differences in the Protestant churches are mostly in their rules of behavior for their members, the rules for holding church services, and in varying ways of admitting new people to membership. All, however, have in common a great body of belief and custom.

Early Maryland Churches and Ministers

Much has been written about members of the Roman Catholic Church who helped to settle Maryland. It is important to understand their contribution to the history of our state. We must, however, not forget the contribution of other religious groups who also did well here. About 34% of all Maryland citizens today are members of Protestant churches, while about 24% belong to the Roman Catholic Church, and another 10% are of the Hebrew faith. The remainder belong to other religious groups or to no specific church at all.[2]

Possibly the very first minister in Maryland was one representing the Church of England, the Reverend Richard James, who joined Captain William Claiborne on Kent Island in 1633. Captain Claiborne, you will remember, was the Virginian who had a trading post on the island as early as 1631.

When colonists sent by Lord Baltimore settled at St. Mary's City in 1634, members of both the Roman Catholic Church and those of the Protestant faith set up places of worship. You will remember that with the *Ark* and the *Dove* were two Jesuit priests, Fathers Andrew White and John Altham. By 1638 there were five Jesuits in Maryland.

In 1648 and 1649 Puritans from Virginia came to Maryland, with Lord Baltimore's permission, and settled on the Severn River near the present site of Annapolis. Puritans were those people who, in the time of Queen Elizabeth I and the first two Stuart rulers of England, opposed the traditional religious forms and wanted simpler church services and customs. As Puritans had done when they gained control of the government in England, in Maryland they also enforced their own kind of toleration—and were most intolerant of Catholicism! They forced Catholics to abandon public religious services and they also denied Catholics many religious, educational, and political rights. If Catholic parents were able to afford the expense, sons of these families were sometimes sent abroad to be educated.

Quakers in Maryland were to speak out for freedom for black men and women.

It is not quite certain when the first Quakers arrived in Maryland, but they were active here by the late 1650's. As early as 1661 "meetings" of the Society of Friends were being organized in Maryland. One of the English founders of the denomination, George Fox, visited Maryland in 1672 and began the "Maryland Yearly Meeting." This was the second such "meeting" set up in America. William Penn, himself a member of the Society of Friends, visited with a congregation on the shores of the Choptank River in December, 1682.

One may still see the Third Haven Meeting House, near Easton, Maryland, on the Eastern Shore. It was constructed in the years 1682-1684 and is said to be the oldest surviving wooden church in the United States.

Wenlock Christison, a pioneer advocate of religious freedom, lived in Talbot County. The story of his experiences in Massachusetts and his coming to Maryland reveals the religious intolerance of that time. He had been persecuted for his beliefs in England, and then, later on, in New England. There, in the 1650's, the Society of Friends were not allowed their own worship. Wenlock Christison was given twenty-seven "cruel stripes" on his bare body for speaking out for his Quaker beliefs.

Christison was turned out of prison at Plymouth, Massachusetts. It was midwinter, and he shivered in his thin clothing as he made his way to Boston. But there he found no haven either. He was told that he must leave and that if he returned he would be executed for being a Quaker. Stubbornly he returned and stubbornly he refused to change his religious principles. He was brought to trial for this before the Governor of Massachusetts and said ". . . I refuse not to die!" The judges and the Governor, though they did not execute him, were determined to humiliate him. He was tied to a cart and made to walk behind it with two other Quakers and was "whipped through three towns."

Christison eventually came to Maryland. Here he was given land for a plantation in Talbot County by Dr. Peter Sharp, a Calvert County physician. In Maryland he became quite active in politics and finally had found a place where he was to be able to live in peace. Christison died in 1679.

Presbyterians

The Reverend Francis Makemie came to the lower Eastern Shore of Maryland in 1683. He founded the first Presbyterian congregations in America.[3] These first church groups were located at Rehoboth, Snow Hill and at the (now) Pocomoke City. In all a total of five congregations were formed by Reverend Makemie and included others at Wicomico and Princess Anne. At Rehoboth, Maryland, one may see a square brick church on the banks of the Pocomoke River. It is said to be the first Presbyterian Church built in America.

Among the Presbyterians, children sat with their parents in church and took part in the services. The sermons were very long and were made to seem even longer because the early churches were unheated in winter. It was not until the early nineteenth century, around 1820, that the idea of having a Sunday School for young people was developed in Maryland. The idea appears to have been first used that year, at the Falling Waters Presbyterian Church, originally founded in Virginia in 1745. This congregation is presently located near Spring Mills in Maryland. The minister's mother put the idea into practice.

Though a Reverend Hugh Conn worked in the North Point area of Baltimore County in 1715, it was not until 1761 that a Presbyterian congregation was organized in Baltimore by Scotch and Irish merchants of that city.

The Presbyterian Church showed new patterns for that time. Henry H. Garnet, who was born in 1815 into slavery on the Eastern Shore of Maryland in Kent County, was brought north when his entire family managed to escape. His study and work resulted in 1842, in his being ordained to the Presbyterian ministry. He was much later appointed as the United States Minister to Liberia in the 1880's. Unfortunately he died there shortly after his arrival.

Old Trinity Church

A beautiful Maryland church and one of the first Protestant churches built in the Province is Old Trinity. It is located not far from Cambridge, on Church Creek in Dorchester County. It is considered to be one of the three oldest church buildings in the United States, which is still in its original form and used regularly. It was built before 1690, although the exact date is not known. The church records were destroyed by fire. Missing from the original equipment of Old Trinity, too, is a very old Bible and a communion set sent to Maryland by Queen Anne of England. The Queen's chalice, however, still remains.

The work of restoring the church was begun in 1953. It was then crumbling away, as might be expected, because of its great age. The efforts and generosity of the Old Trinity Association, and that of

Colonel and Mrs. Edgar W. Garbisch, carried the work through to completion in 1960.

In the churchyard of Old Trinity are the graves of Maryland's former Governor, Thomas King Carroll, as well as those of his son, Maryland's "beloved physician," Dr. Thomas King Carroll; and of his daughter, Anna Ella Carroll. Here also are the graves of several officers who served in the American Revolution.

The Roman Catholic Church

The Lord Proprietary gave orders strictly forbidding religious arguments aboard the *Ark* and the *Dove*, as the colonists came out to Maryland. After the settlement was begun at St. Mary's City there was unusual religious toleration during the first years.

By the early 1700's, things had changed. There was still toleration in Maryland for members of some Protestant churches, but members of the Roman Catholic Church were unfairly treated in many ways. Catholic priests were forbidden to hold public worship and were not supposed to baptise children into the Catholic faith! All members of the Roman Catholic Church by 1740 were required to pay double taxes; and Catholics were largely prevented by law from holding public office and from voting, thanks to a 1718 ruling. Now a part of this oppression was due to the Protestants' dislike of Catholicism itself, or "Popery" as they called it; and part was due to the fact that Catholics were thought to favor the Stuart family of English royalty, which by that time had been driven from the throne.

Because of this treatment, Catholic priests and church members avoided public worship. They "went underground"—attending services held privately in homes or in other convenient, non-public places. As late as 1800 it is estimated that there were less than 3,000 Catholics and only a half-dozen Jesuit priests in Maryland.

Early Catholic Churches

The Jesuits had a brick chapel on their land at their headquarters on St. Thomas Manor, and at St. Inigoes Manor, in St. Mary's County. Little chapels of worship were set up in the homes of the wealthier Catholics. The more wealth a Catholic might have, the finer chapel he could build. There was, for example, an elaborate and lovely chapel built earlier in 1636, at St. Mary's City. This is today possibly the oldest Catholic church site in all of the thirteen original colonies, as well as the oldest in the country in continuous possession by the

Jesuits. When, in 1704, Catholics were forbidden to worship publicly, "St. Maries" was closed and its bricks removed to other Jesuit property. In 1785 land for a new church was selected and the present church was completed in 1788. This Catholic shrine has one of our nation's oldest cemeteries beside it. The men of the nearby Patuxent Naval Air Test Center, together with residents of St. Mary's County, have been working since 1950 to restore the church.

Maryland has a rich Catholic religious heritage. The first American bishop of the Roman Catholic Church was the Right Reverend John Carroll of Maryland. He was consecrated Bishop in 1790, with a diocese that then included the entire United States!

Bishop Carroll invited priests to come to Baltimore in order to plan the first English-speaking seminary—a school for training candidates for the priesthood. In 1808 the cornerstone was laid for what became St. Mary's Chapel on Paca Street in Baltimore. Hidden away and scarcely known to the public, this little chapel is a gem of early architecture and is still used by priests and seminarians.

Just outside the walls of St. Mary's Chapel, Mother Seton's "Sisters of Charity" order was founded. There her first school for children was started. She later moved her school to Emmittsburg, Maryland, where she was made the Mother Superior of her order of nuns. This order is known today as the "Daughters of Charity in the United States." Mother Seton was beatified by the Pope of the Roman Catholic Church in 1963.

The oldest convent in America is located near La Plata and Port Tobacco, in Charles County. It is called Mount Carmel and was established in 1790. Carmelite nuns came first to Chandler's Hope, a large home near Port Tobacco, but on October 15 of that year they moved to the nearby Mount Carmel location. The order was begun by three Charles County women of the Matthews family who were members of the Carmelite order, and by a fourth nun, an Englishwoman. The Americans had gone to Belgium originally to take orders as nuns and had then returned to their native America.

These four nuns stayed at Mount Carmel for forty-one years and then at the invitation of Bishop Carroll they moved in 1831, to Baltimore. The Mount Carmel convent and chapel are being restored by a group formed in 1935—called the Restorers of Mount Carmel. Seven acres of land have been purchased surrounding the restored convent buildings for the purpose of creating this historic shrine honoring the first order of nuns in the United States.

Church of the Redeemer   (Maryland Dept. of Economic Development)

Charles Randolph Uncles

America's first black Catholic priest was ordained in December of 1891. His name was Charles Randolph Uncles. He was born in Baltimore and first baptised in 1875 at St. Francis Xavier Church and confirmed in 1878. This is the oldest American church serving a black congregation.

The St. Francis Xavier Church had a profound influence on the young Baltimore man. The congregation of the church had organized as far back as 1798. The church itself was organized in 1863. It was one of Baltimore's leading black houses of worship. The location is 1007 North Caroline Street.

Most Catholic churches have an important percentage of black members. Also, several black priests have been ordained in Maryland and a number are at work in the various Catholic parishes of the state. In recent years, older separations of the races have been removed and the trend is for persons of all races to be welcome. Catholic schools have long been open to all children of Catholic persuasion, regardless of racial background.

44

Mother Mary Elizabeth Lange, foundress of the Oblate Sisters of Providence. The present headquarters of this religious order are located on a 46-acre site on Gun Road, south of Catonsville.

Illustration courtesy Oblate Sisters of Providence, Baltimore, Maryland.

Her parents left Haiti for Cuba in the early 1800s. Later, she and her mother came to the United States. The young Elizabeth Lange managed to obtain an excellent education, although we do not know just how. We do know that she spoke both French and English.

In Maryland, Elizabeth Lange noticed that young black girls had little chance for an education. They had even less chance than the white girls who could, if family finances permitted, obtain a little schooling at small schools. Elizabeth Lange decided to correct this situation by starting a school for black girls. Most of the students came from the congregation of St. Mary's Seminary Chapel, a church serving the black immigrants who shared the French language. By 1827, however, Miss Lange had to close the school for lack of funds.

She spoke to the Surplician fathers who had established the Chapel. A school is so badly needed, she explained. Also, she told Father James Joubet, who took an interest in her work, she had another desire, to become a Catholic nun. (At the time there were no Catholic orders accepting black women.)

Elizabeth Lange and Father Joubet agreed on two important steps; to establish a religious order, a teaching order of nuns, for black women. This would, in turn, make it possible to start and maintain a Catholic school for black girls. The Archbishop of Baltimore was asked for his approval. He liked the idea and gave his consent.

In June, 1828, Miss Lange and two friends began their novitiate. This is a period of training and one in which a girl wishing to become a nun discovers whether or not she is suited for a religious life. Miss Lange was named Superior, and was the leader of the very small new order. They named their order the Oblate Sisters of Providence.

Now, near Paca Street in Baltimore, the women opened their school. Many of their pupils were daughters of French-speaking refugees from the Caribbean.

After taking their first vows on July 2, 1829, the Sisters looked for a safer and more permanent location for their growing school. A patron (one who donates money or services) sold them a house on Pennsylvania Avenue which the Sisters named Saint Frances Academy.

Upon taking her vows, Elizabeth Lange took the name Sister Mary. Her talents as an executive and as a teacher were impressive. The Oblate order served the community faithfully---teaching, nursing, and comforting persons who sought their help.

By the time of her death in 1882, Sister Mary was very nearly 100 years of age. She had seen much in her busy life. The order she had helped to found was now over fifty years old and was a leader in black education in Baltimore. Sister Mary had seen black Americans freed by the ending of the Civil War. Steady progress continued in Baltimore's black community, helped on by the dedicated services of the Oblate sisters.

The Oblate order and many of the schools the original sisters started, still operate in Baltimore City today.

There are so many beautiful churches in Maryland that the state might easily be known as the land of great churches and of great church history. In fact, there is material for several books just on the denominations and churches of Maryland alone. Mention, of course, should include the first Roman Catholic cathedral in the United States, begun in 1806 in Baltimore. Bishop John Carroll himself laid the cornerstone, at a time when about half of all Roman Catholic Church members in the United States lived in Maryland. Maryland is still a state which is a leader in that church's activities in our nation.

Bishop Carroll was a great and very active churchman, for he helped found the religious order called the Sisters of Charity; and he was a prime mover in founding Georgetown University, in 1791, which was located then in Maryland, but is now in the District of Columbia. Bishop Carroll, who in 1808 became the first Archbishop of Baltimore, died in 1815. He is buried in the cathedral that he helped to build— the Cathedral of the Assumption of the Blessed Virgin Mary, in Baltimore City.

A Washington, D.C. congregation.
Illustrated London News, Nov. 18, 1876.
Photograph courtesy Library of Congress.

Moravian Churches

A spring of fresh, cold water was the reason for locating a church near Graceham, Maryland. The spring allowed church-goers to quench their thirst and provided water for their horses, too. Graceham Moravian Church was begun by Jacob Weller not long after he arrived in Maryland, about 1742. On the same site occupied by today's church, the first Moravian church in Maryland was built in 1749.

The first Moravians to come to America settled in Pennsylvania about 1741. They were of German background and they believed in living lives of goodness and simplicity. They brought with them "brass choirs." In 1752 trombones were added to the other brass instruments in these choirs. It is an unusual and very vigorous kind of church music. It can be heard today at the mother church in Bethlehem, Pennsylvania, and on occasion, at Graceham Moravian Church in Maryland.

The Protestant Episcopal Church
(Formerly the Church of England)

An Anglican clergyman, the Reverend William Wilkinson came to the Province of Maryland, probably in the year 1658. He preached to a congregation which was to become the St. George's Poplar Grove Parish in St. Mary's County. This gives that Anglican church a good claim to being the oldest in Maryland[4] for it was founded shortly after the founding of Lord Baltimore's colony.[5] Earlier a Protestant group had built a chapel in the county, but it was not at first served by a minister. Thomas Gerard, a Catholic, in 1642 was found guilty and fined 500 pounds of tobacco, for taking the key and books of a Protestant chapel located on his land. This tobacco money was ordered to be set aside to help support the first Protestant minister who should come to Maryland.

Under the Royal government of Maryland an act was passed in the Assembly in 1692 to establish the Church of England, sometimes called the Anglican Church, as the official religion of the colony. Thirty parishes were laid out. A tax to support this church was placed on everyone regardless of his religion.

It was in this same year that St. Anne's Church in Annapolis was founded. King William III of England presented communion silver to St. Anne's, and it is still there in use today. When one visits Annapolis he will see the present church structure, built on the site of the original St. Anne's. This building is made of red brick of a warm, rosy shade and is gracefully proportioned. To the left of the entrance there is a marble slab whose faded carving reads: "Here lieth interred the body of Mr. Amos Garrett, merchant, chosen first Mayor of Annapolis . . . Born 1671 in Southwark, London, England. Died in Annapolis on the 8th of March 1727 at the age of 56."

The Reverend Thomas Bray, Commissary of the Church of England, in 1699 collected books to form parish libraries and to start a central Anglican library in Annapolis. He came to Maryland to help in the development of the young parishes in the province.

The Anglican Church was disestablished, that is, it was declared to be no longer the official church of Maryland under the provisions of the first State Constitution of Maryland in December, 1776. This

The first St. Anne's Church, Annapolis, Maryland. Sketch from Elisabeth L. Ridout collection.
Maryland Hall of Records.

left the former Church of England parishes in a sort of legal vacuum. So the property and operation of the church were made the responsibility of eight men from each parish. The Vestry Act of 1779 set up certain legal procedures for what had formerly been the official church. It provided for giving to the members of the former State Church the church property; and the management of the church was placed in the hands of an elected group of persons, the "vestry." The members of the vestry were to be elected each Easter Sunday by the church members.

A new name for the former Church of England in America was decided upon at a conference held in 1783 in Chestertown, Maryland. The church would now be the Protestant Episcopal Church. The Reverend Thomas John Claggett of Maryland was chosed to be the first bishop of the newly reorganized church. He was consecrated in 1792.

In Cecil County, Maryland, Bishop Stone ordained in June, 1834, the first black to be a Deacon in the Episcopal Church, not only in Maryland but in the entire South. The man so chosen was William Douglass. The Bishop praised Douglass for the sermon he gave to church members. Later, on February 14, 1836, Douglass became a priest of the Episcopal Church. In the years that followed he wrote a book of sermons and a church history. For twenty-seven years he

49

worked as the minister of St. Thomas (African) Church in Philadelphia. He was born in Baltimore in 1805 and died May 22, 1862.

Another prominent black Marylander, the Reverend Doctor George F. Bragg was to serve that same Philadelphia church for fifty years. Reverend Bragg wrote a book titled *Men of Maryland*, published in 1914.

Baptists

In a walnut and oak grove on Chestnut Ridge in Howard County is the first Baptist church built in Maryland. After meeting for a time at the home of Henry Sater, the congregation with Sater's aid built a brick church on land Sater had donated in 1742. The church is called, not surprisingly, "Sater's Baptist Church." The deed to the congregation states that the land was donated for a meeting house and burying ground, ". . . .forever to the end of the world." The Baptist Church was a popular one in the state and its membership grew.

In 1835 the Reverend Moses Clayton, a black minister, came to Baltimore to found a Baptist Church in that city. It was February, 1836 that he organized what was to be the First Baptist Church. The growth of that church continued, particularly under the direction of Reverend Harvey Johnson in the 1870's.

The Lutheran Church

As early as 1729 some of the German settlers coming to Maryland from Pennsylvania were members of the Lutheran and Reformed churches. These people were Germans only in the sense that all of them spoke the German language. At that time there was no united Germany as we know it today. Both of these German denominations at first used a single church building near Creagerstown, Maryland. Later the Reformed Church congregation moved to Frederick and that city has become a center of Reformed Church activity.

In Baltimore the first Lutheran Reformed Church congregation worshipped as early as 1756 in the "town clock church." Dr. Wiesenthal, an early Maryland leader in medicine and anatomical research, was prominently identified with Baltimore's Lutheran beginnings.

The Methodist Church

Today some of the Methodist churches in Maryland are reviving the practice, on occasion, of holding services at the edge of Chesapeake Bay with a minister speaking from a boat to the people on the shore. This practice began with the early preaching of Robert Strawbridge who, about 1760, preached some sermons in this way in the Annapolis area. The first Methodist place of worship in Maryland is where the Reverend Strawbridge preached in a small log chapel on Sam's Creek in Carroll County.

Organized Methodism in America dates from the year 1771, when Reverend Francis Asbury began his work in the United States. In Baltimore he succeeded in getting a meeting house built in the year 1773. Construction of the Lovely Lane Meeting House was started in 1774. Baltimore has always been an important center of Methodism. In the large Lovely Lane church in Baltimore, there is a section devoted to the historic papers and objects relating to the history of Methodism in America. Lovely Lane Museum is located on St. Paul Street and is open to the public.

So many Marylanders came to support the Methodist Church, that our state was often referred to as the "Garden of Methodism."

One of the early Methodist workers on the Eastern Shore was Joshua Thomas. He came to be called the "Parson of the Islands." He was born in Somerset County in 1776 and grew up in poverty

Forrest Stith, chief executive officer of the United Methodist Baltimore Conference, which includes the District of Columbia, leads delegates in hymn singing at the United Methodist General Conerence in Indianapolis.

Washington Star

on the islands of the lower Chesapeake Bay. While visiting a camp meeting of Methodists in 1807 the young fisherman became converted to Methodism and was soon a Methodist "exhorter." In 1814 he became a local preacher. It was in this year that he accurately predicted that the British fleet attacking Baltimore would be defeated. Parson Thomas died in 1853 after many years of preaching. He is buried beside the Deal Island Methodist Episcopal Church, located in the lower Bay area.

Methodism appealed to both white and black people. Several prominent Methodist preachers in Maryland were black men. The first society of black Methodists was orgnized about 1797 and was served by a black minister, Daniel Coker. Born in Frederick County in the latter part of the eighteenth century, he was one of those ministers ordained by Bishop Asbury. He worked in Baltimore and helped in the organization of the Sharp Street Methodist Church (1802) and operated a very famous church school, which was often called "Dan Coker's School." He was a leader, too, in the Philadelphia convention which resulted in the organization of the African Methodist Episcopal Church in 1816. He was elected to be its first bishop but decided to decline that post. Reverend Coker left America in 1820 for Liberia and later went to Sierra Leone where he built a church and raised his family.

Shown here is the Chapel of the University of Maryland, College Park Campus.

When the American Revolution split American churches away from their home church headquarters in Europe, there followed a time of confusion. The leaders of the Methodist Church, in 1784, in a Christmas conference in Baltimore, gathered at the Lovely Lane Meeting House. There the separate churches were merged into one national body, known now as the Methodist Episcopal Church.

During the Civil War the Methodist church again found itself divided. The churches split on a North and South basis and it was to be many years before they began to draw together again. In 1939 all were reunited under the original name, the Methodist Church. This church was to merge with another denomination in the late 1960's to become the United Methodist Church.

An unusual Methodist church is the one called the Stone Chapel, located just off Reisterstown Road in Baltimore County. It is of Greek Doric design and was completed in 1862. Its congregation first met in the home of Joshua Owings. Then a first stone chapel was built on ground bought in 1785. It is said that the son of Joshua Owings was the first native American to be ordained a Methodist minister in the United States.

Hebrew Congregations

There were apparently few Jewish people in Maryland in colonial times. However, there is seldom to be found any record of actual persecution of this religious group. Laws in Maryland did definitely favor members of the Christian religions. Jews who were members of the Hebrew congregations were prohibited from voting or holding public office in Maryland until 1825.

The Baltimore Hebrew Congregation was chartered in 1829, and in 1838 the Fells Point Hebrew Friendship Congregation was started. Today almost every Maryland community of any size has a Hebrew temple, and many of the leaders of our state are of Hebrew family background.

Religion in Maryland Today

There have been mentioned here only some of the larger denominations in Maryland. There are many other religious groups with very interesting histories. Our state is rich in unique places of worship.

Two sects that have emerged with Maryland connections and that have won national attention are those of George Baker and G. M. Grace. George Baker became known as the head of a large church and was nationally known as Father Divine. G. M. Grace was called Bishop Grace, or Father Grace, and headed missions of his religious group in various parts of the country. Both of these religious organizations were most active in the 1940's.

A great deal has been written about historic church buildings, yet surviving more strongly than the buildings are the congregations themselves. People hand down their faith, their hopes, their ideals, and their responsibilities to the generations following them. In religious life as in our secular lives, we today learn from past events and in turn hand our hopes and beliefs down to succeeding generations.

---

1 The Holy Orthodox Catholic Apostolic Eastern Church is another title of the Orthodox Church.
2 **The Statesman's Year Book: 1968-69,** p. 687.
3 These were the first regularly constituted Presbyterian congregations. There is some evidence of still earlier Presbyterian activity in Charles County between 1658 and 1662.
4 **Maryland Historical Magazine,** XXI, No. 1, March 1926.
5 The student must keep in mind the fact that an Anglican minister, the Reverend Richard James was at the Kent Island post with William Claiborne prior to the time of Lord Baltimore's St. Mary's City settlement; and it is thought that he was the first Anglican to preach in Maryland.

Recommended reading:
Maryland Historical Magazine, Volume XXI, No. 1, March 1926, the article by Bernard C. Steiner, "Maryland's Religious History."

No one knows what he can do till he tries.

Publicus Syrus

CHAPTER VIII

NOTED MARYLAND MEN AND WOMEN: 1700 — 1900

Following are brief biographies of some of Maryland's many gifted black men and women. There were, of course, many others whose stories are not told. This does not, however, make their work less important to the progress of Maryland and the nation. While remembering those men and women whose stories appear below, we also remember that each citizen of Maryland is a part of the growth and well-being of our state, whether or not histories tell their stories.

Joshua Johnston

One of the best known black portrait artists of the 1700s and early 1800s was Joshua Johnston of Baltimore. It is believed that Johnston was either born a free man, or earned his freedom through his painting skills. In any case, he lived in Baltimore City and was actively at work from around 1765 to 1830.

About two dozen of his paintings have been located by the Maryland Historical Society. The paintings capture likenesses yet are in the two-dimensional style of colonial portraitists, or "limners," as they were called. Johnston no doubt learned most of his skills by himself. His work has a warmth and charm that many other early American artists lack.

For over thirty years he lived at various addresses in Baltimore City and painted portraits of the members of wealthy families for a living. Clients may have come to his studio at times, for often his pictures show the same handsome sofa and the pictures often include the portrait of an odd-looking little white dog.

Examples of Johnston's work are exhibited at the Maryland Historical Society.

Education is an ornament in prosperity and a refuge in adversity.
Aristotle

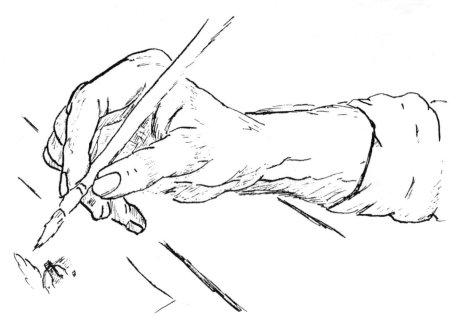

Ira Aldridge

It seems that persons who excel in America, are those who seek out education. Perhaps their minds are as hungry for learning new things as their bodies are interested in good food. This seems to be the case in the story of Ira Aldridge who was born about 1805 and grew up in Bel Air, Maryland.

As soon as he could he went to New York and attended the African Free School there. There were almost no black schools in Maryland in the early 1800s. Next, Aldridge went to the Schenectady College in New York state. It was there that he discovered his talents as an actor.

This was what he wanted to do! But how? There was little chance of his playing the important dramatic parts he was interested in in the United States. Somehow he raised money to get to Scotland, a brave move for a young American at that time. He went on with his education at the University of Glasgow. There he developed the accent, the voice projection and dramatic skills that were to serve him well. Actors must not only develop their minds, however, they must use their bodies in portraying their parts. Aldridge walked for miles in the raw Scottish mists, practiced fencing and developed the broad physique that commanded attention on the stage. He won academic honors at the University. He was now ready to work in the theater.

By 1833, Aldridge was drawing crowds to see his portrayal of Shakespearean roles. In Ireland and later, in Europe, Aldridge's acting fascinated audiences. He was decorated by princes and kings. The heads of state decorated him for his exciting Shakespearean roles.

If you visit Stratford-on-Avon in England, you may see the Shakespearean Memorial Theater there. In his memory an Ira Aldridge chair is designated for him in that theater.

All his life he kept his head, striving to never grow too proud to learn more and to marvel at all he saw. He died in 1867, honored all across Europe.

Frederick Douglass

One of the most distinguished of Marylanders was Frederick Douglass. He was born into slavery in Talbot County, Maryland, in 1817. He was of both black and white ancestry. As a child he was starved and ill-treated by a slavewoman, "Aunt Katy." This treatment was allowed by his master. He once saw an overseer shoot and kill a black man when the man plunged into a creek to escape a whipping. For Douglass, injustice and cruelty darkened many of his boyhood days. He grew tall and strong and, at the age of sixteen, he objected to a whipping. He was sent to Baltimore and hired out by his master there to work on the Baltimore docks. He turned most of his

Frederick Douglass.

courtesy U.S. Parks Service

wages over to his master. He longed to learn to read and while he was in Baltimore he did manage to do so. He treasured the one ragged book on oratory (public speaking) that he owned. At the age of twenty-one he escaped to the North.

In the North he improved his education and rapidly grew to be a famous speaker, author, and later on, a newspaper editor. His work was directed toward the improvement of the life of black people and, of course, he worked for the abolition of slavery. All of his life, in fact, he worked for the freedom of blacks but steadfastly refused to advise the use of force or violence to bring this about.

This remarkable man, in time became a United States Marshall; and he served for a time as the United States' Minister to Haiti. Also, in another period, he served as Recorder of Deeds in the District of Columbia. He made his home, during his last years, on an estate called Cedar Hill in Washington. Many people came to him there for advice and help. He died in 1895.

The Douglass Home.   Open to the public.

courtesy U.S. Parks Service

Benjamin Banneker

Matthew Henson

Frances E. W. Harper

James W. C. Pennington

The story of Benjamin Banneker (1731-1806) has been given earlier in this work. He became, you may remember, a well-known almanac author, a surveyor, an inventor, and an astronomer. Also, in a later chapter the life of yet another important Marylander will be presented, that of the adventures of Matthew Henson, the Arctic explorer (1866-1955). Another prominent black Marylander was Frances E. W. Harper (1825-1911). She was a lecturer and a member of the powerful Women's Christian Temperance Union movement. Still another well-known representative of the black Marylander, was James W. C. Pennington (1809-1870), who was born a slave on the Eastern Shore of Maryland, and who, after his escape to freedom became an outstanding preacher, and author.

Harriet Tubman

In some respects the most remarkable of these black leaders and the subject of several books was Harriet Tubman (1815-1913). She escaped from an Eastern Shore plantation when she was twenty-five years of age. She decided to help others escape, too. It is said that

"On my Underground Railroad
I never ran my train off the track
And I never lost a passenger."

she led over three hundred people to freedom. So effective was this Maryland woman that a reward of $40,000 was offered for her capture! During the Civil War she had further adventures as a nurse and a secret Union agent. Later she helped many blacks to obtain schooling and was always ready to extend a helping hand. One of the last things she did before she died was to found a home for the aged. She had spent her lifetime in remarkable services for her people.

Josiah Henson

Another able spokesman for freedom was Josiah Henson (1789-1883), who was born a slave in Charles County, Maryland. In 1828 he became a preacher and was an outstanding worker and supervisor on the plantation where he lived. Like so many blacks, he had become convinced that to be successful he must give loyal and diligent service to his owner. At last, however, he realized that slavery was not a duty, nor an obligation to be endured permanently. He crossed into Canada in 1830. Eventually he was to tell his story to the famous writer, Harriet Beecher Stowe. Henson is thought by many to have been the character called "Uncle Tom," in her novel, *Uncle Tom's Cabin*, published in 1853. This book was widely read and did a great deal to stir up public opinion against the practice of slavery in the United States. Henson preached, lectured, and wrote for many years.

JOSIAH HENSON (1789-1883). He escaped from bondage in Maryland and became a well known Methodist preacher and an author. He is said to have been the model for Uncle Tom, in Uncle Tom's Cabin.

He came to be known and loved as Father Josiah Henson. He published autobiographical books in 1849, 1858, and 1879.

Dreaming men are haunted men.

Stephen Vincent Benet

CHAPTER IX

MATTHEW HENSON AT THE NORTH POLE

A PRIL 6 is set aside in Maryland as the official Matthew Henson Day. But who was Matthew Henson and what happened on April 6th? This is our story in this chapter. It is a tale of action, danger and adventure.

Matthew Henson was born on his father's farm in Charles County, Maryland, on August 8, 1866. The black family was threatened by an illegal band of terrorists called the Klu Klux Klan, and were forced to sell their farm and move away. Matt was quite small when they made the move from Charles County to Washington, D.C. Matt grew up there in the Georgetown section. His mother died while he was very little, and his father entrusted him to the care of an uncle. By the time he had completed the sixth grade in school, however, he was homeless and had to go to work in a small restaurant in order to eat. He stayed there for just a short time, sleeping on the floor at night. Then Matt decided that he would seek work and adventure on the sea. He walked all the way to Baltimore and began to stay around the waterfront. Until the mid-1800's many ships were propelled by sails. In Baltimore Matt found a place as a cabin boy on a sailing ship.

The captain of the ship liked Matt, taught him mathematics and navigation and let Matt read books in the captain's cabin. Matt soon learned all of the skills of the sailor, too. He learned how to climb into the rigging and to operate the lines that operated the huge sails. He learned how to do the many things necessary to help keep the ship seaworthy. It was a hard life, but one in which Matt took great pride.

Matthew Henson became an able seaman while still in his teens. He sailed for five years aboard the *Katie Hines* and saw many exotic world ports. In 1885, following the death of the captain of the ship, to whom the youngster was devoted, he left the *Katie Hines* and decided reluctantly to seek work ashore. He was now a master mechanic and a good carpenter, and he hoped to find steady employment.

Unfortunately for Matt, finding a good job was not easy. He even went to Buffalo, New York, and worked there as a night watchman. Later on he tried several other jobs, but found none very interesting or rewarding. Finally he came back to Washington, D. C. and became

Matthew Henson (1866-1955) Arctic explorer.

a helper in a store which sold men's hats and furs. Here he met a young Navy lieutenant, Robert E. Peary. Peary asked Henson to go with him to Nicaragua in Central America, as his valet. Matt liked the idea of adventure overseas. So, in November, 1887, they left New York.

The purpose of the Nicaraguan expedition was to finish surveying a mid-American canal route. The proposed canal was to extend from the Atlantic to the Pacific through Nicaragua, to allow ships to sail from ocean to ocean without going all the way around South America first. This was, of course, long before the building of the Panama Canal. Once there and at work, Henson was soon asked to leave his duties as valet and become a member of the survey crew. Again, the work was not easy, but it was important and interesting, and Henson liked that. In the summer of 1888, Peary and Henson were back in the United States. Henson renewed his search for an interesting job. Peary asked Henson to keep in touch with him.

A year or so went by and then Peary contacted Henson. Peary wanted Henson to go with him on an exploring expedition to the icy waters and highlands of Greenland. This was the Peary expedition of 1891-1892. Again, in the years 1893-1895 Henson was asked to go with Peary on other Greenland expeditions. Though called Peary's manservant, actually Henson was an invaluable and loyal aide. Henson mastered the art of driving a team of dogs hitched to a sled. Sleds pulled by dog teams provided the best means of transportation over the ice and snow in Arctic regions. The Eskimoes in the region thought of Henson as one of themselves because of his dark skin. He had an unusual talent for making friends with the Eskimo people and he learned to speak their language well. He learned from them how to make igloos of ice and snow as well as ways of building and repairing the dog sleds. He was devoted to Peary and became expert in the techniques of exploration of Arctic areas. Always, when Peary asked for volunteers for difficult tasks, Henson stepped forward. In the art of staying alive and traveling in the Arctic, Henson excelled. Peary explored Greenland for several years, learning for one thing that it was an island and not part of an Arctic mainland. In the ten years between 1892 and 1902, Peary made many trips into the Arctic, aspiring now to be the first man to reach the North Pole. Henson was always included on these expeditions. After the end of the expedition of 1902, Henson, liking the travel involved, worked as a porter on a railroad. During these years he met a young woman, Lucy Ross, while visiting in Chicago. They became engaged to be married. But, before this could take place, Peary called for Henson again for his 1905 expedition. This Arctic exploration was aimed straight for the North Pole! In 1902, Peary and Henson had gotten

Matthew A. Henson, 1910. A George Bain photograph.
Library of Congress.

further north in the Western Hemisphere (84°16°27″) than any other men. On that expedition, Peary had finally turned back sadly feeling, at age forty-six and after sixteen years of Arctic exploration, that he would never reach his great goal. Peary hoped to achieve for the United States and for himself the distinction of being the first to reach "the top of the world."

With Peary, now nearing fifty years of age, on his 1905-1906 expedition were three other white men and Henson. Matt was thirty-nine years old at this time. The expedition leader planned to use his carefully-thought-out "Peary system." This involved getting as far north as possible in the ice-breaker ship the *S.S. Roosevelt*, then sending out teams of men with dogs and sleds to clear a trail and to set up igloos with caches of food and fuel. Peary and his team of five men were to follow and in this way would be fresh enough to make that last dash for the North Pole. Open gaps, or leads of deep black water lay between them and their goal. These had to close together in time, or else Peary, Henson, and the four Eskimo men with them would not have time and supplies to reach the Pole and still return alive to the ship. On this expedition Peary reached a north point of 87°6′, farther north than any other man had ever gotten. But, then weather and open water stopped him from reaching the North Pole.

In 1908, yet another expedition set out. Once more Henson went with Peary, and again the "Peary system" was put into practice. The commander was now a Navy Admiral. The weather and the water conditions were a bit more favorable this time. Months and years of planning and effort were finally beginning to count in their favor when, on April 4, 1909, an advance group, consisting of the Admiral, Henson, and four Eskimo men, found themselves just sixty miles from the North Pole. In the next two days they overcame seemingly impossible problems, and arrived on April 6, 1909, at 89 degrees 57 minutes 11 seconds. . .about three nautical miles from the Pole. Camp was made here and Peary, accompanied by two of the Eskimoes went on some ten miles further for another reading. The sextent showed that the party had passed the Pole. They made their way back and forth across the area several times and took other sextant readings to be sure that "at some moment during these marches and countermarches I had passed over or very near the point where north and south and east and west blend into one."[1]

Back at the camp site Peary handed Matthew Henson the flag of the United States and Henson planted it firmly in place, within sight of the North Pole. Peary took pictures of Matt and the Eskimo men. On their return trip, the open leads of water, for a change, were a minor problem, and storms held off. They regained land and the

Admiral Robert E. Peary on the *Roosevelt*, 1909.
Library of Congress

Admiral wrote in his diary: "My life work is accomplished." After twenty-three years of effort the prize was won for Peary and his men, and for the United States.

After their return from the North Pole, Henson seldom saw his commander except to receive orders from him. Admiral Peary was honored for his great explorations. Another explorer later claimed to have been the first to reach the Pole, and this tended for a time to dim Peary's triumph, but the claim was later found to be untrue.

It has been said that Henson was neglected by Peary after the Polar expedition. It is true that the two men were estranged when Henson made a lecture tour soon after his return. Peary felt that Henson was included in the agreement he had made with the other men which gave Peary the only rights to speaking and publishing the story of the expedition. Henson had not signed any agreement, however, and so believed that he might lecture and write freely. Peary had been ambitious all his life to become famous and he did not like to share the honor of reaching the Pole. Yet Henson had always been loyal to his old friend and had given up much to go with Peary and had been his staunch and enduring companion through all the northern travels. Fortunately, later on the two were again on friendly terms, although they did not meet again for some years. The Admiral

wrote a preface to the book that Henson wrote, *A Negro Explorer at the North Pole*, published in 1912. An author's study of Peary's papers, made recently, revealed also that Peary wrote several letters of recommendation for Henson.

There had been a deep bond between the two men, though at that time there was a great difference in station between an Admiral and a black aide. In 1920 when Peary lay on his deathbed, he sent for Henson. Henson went to him and they talked together at last. Not long after Henson's visit, Peary died. When Henson heard of Peary's death, he went into another room so that his wife, Lucy, would not see him weep.

Though honored by members of his own race, Matthew Henson was to live for twenty-eight years quietly, almost unknown to the public. But Henson was not discouraged. He worked at a Customs House post that an explorer companion obtained for him. He felt that one day his work would be recognized. Once Henson said to Lowell Thomas, the world-roving writer and radio reporter, "History will take care of that. God will see to it, and God has plenty of helpers." Little did Henson know that a helper was to work most of his life to see that Henson's work was known. That helper was Herbert M. Frisby of Baltimore, Maryland.

Frisby, now Dr. Herbert M. Frisby was born and raised in a slum section of Baltimore. He worked his way through elementary and high school and then through Howard, Columbia, and New York Universities, as well as other graduate schools. Dr. Frisby had learned as a boy of the black who was member of the Peary expedition. "I'm going to be the second black to go to the North Pole," the boy had exclaimed; and forty years later he actually was to realize that ambition. All his life Dr. Frisby worked to focus attention upon Henson; and he was able to get Henson recognition while the explorer still lived.

Henson was seventy years old when he retired. At last recognition began to come to him. In 1937 he was selected to be a member of the famous Explorer's Club. In 1945 the Congress of the United States presented him with a silver medal "for contributing materially to the discovery of the North Pole." Henson often dropped in on the Explorer's Club and spent many of the happiest hours of his retirement there. Dr. Frisby went on working, too, in his behalf. When in 1954, Henson was almost eighty-five, he accepted an invitation to go to Washington, D.C., to lay a wreath on Peary's grave. On April 6, of that year, forty-five years after reaching the North Pole, Henson was the guest of President Dwight D. Eisenhower at the White House.

When Henson died in 1955, his wife, Lucy, insisted on giving half of his insurance money to the Explorer's Club. She explained that she wanted the Club to have the money because Henson had spent so many happy hours with the Club members there.

A special mission was flown by a United States Air Force plane,

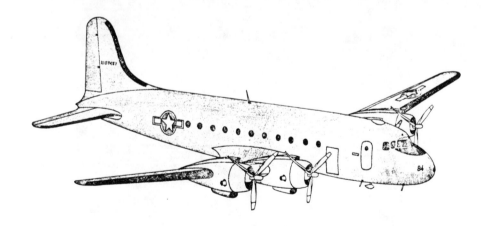

on August 12, 1956, in order to drop a memorial on the North Pole itself in honor of Matthew Henson. Dr. Herbert M. Frisby dropped the memorial, and in so doing realized his boyhood dream of becoming the second black man at the North Pole. Frisby's life has been an adventurous one, modeled after his boyhood hero, Henson. He combined a life of teaching with a life of Arctic travel, most of it at his own expense, and a life of working for recognition for Matthew Henson. Dr. Frisby has completed twenty-two missions into the Arctic and Polar regions, and in the summer of 1970 he was in Russia's Arctic circle area on yet another mission.

Among the honors Dr. Frisby and the people helping him have won for Matthew Henson is a plaque, mounted in the main hall of the beautiful old statehouse in Annapolis, Maryland. Henson's native state honored him in 1961 with formal ceremonies led by Governor J. Millard Tawes and other officials, and attended by Matt's widow, Lucy. On the plaque, Matthew Henson is recognized as "co-discoverer of the North Pole." Maryland also has set aside April 6 as Matthew

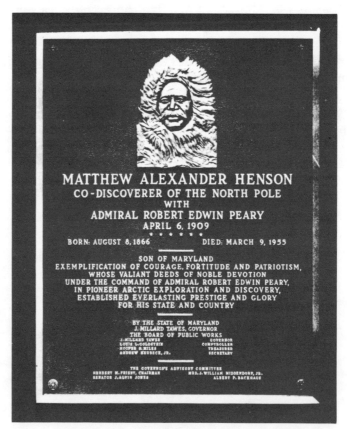

Memorial tablet, located in the State House, Annapolis.
Hall of Records, Dept. of General Services, State of Maryland.

68

Henson Day, and a school in Baltimore City is named for this great explorer.

Henson's recognition, while in no way taking away from the great achievement of Admiral Peary, does recognize Henson's invaluable assistance to Peary. When the team of six men raced back from the Pole over the Polar sea toward land, the exertion and age of Peary showed, and he had to ride the sled frequently. Henson said of that journey later: "(Peary) was practically a dead weight, but I do not think that we could have gotten back without him, for. . .he was still the heart and head of the party." Nor should we forget Peary's efforts at fund-raising, his life of dedication, and the organization and leadership of the man. If he was a bit reluctant to let another in his command enjoy also the lime-light, it is perhaps understandable. Today we honor both men and are proud that it was not one, but two great Americans who went first to the "top of the world."

Henson did not live an easy life, nor did his devoted friend, Dr. Frisby. Yet both men lived happy, adventurous lives. Both men had few advantages in their youth except for their good health and intelligence. But with honest determination, it seems regardless of handicaps, failures and problems, one can reach a goal in life. The story of Peary, Henson and Frisby leaves us with much to admire, and much to think about.

---

1 Peary, **The North Pole**, p. 291.

Dr. Herbert Frisby

There is no hope of joy except in human relations.
                                           Antoine Saint-Exupery

CHAPTER X

MARYLANDERS WHO WORKED FOR CHANGE

From hundreds of noted Maryland citizens who have worked for changes and advancement, the following persons have been chosen. Their representative stories show that one man's or one woman's work *can* make a difference.

The Murphy Family

No story of Maryland history would be complete without mention of a nationally-known family called Murphy. A most important project was begun on August 13, 1892, when a four-page sheet was printed by the Reverend William M. Alexander, pastor of the Sharon Baptist Church in Baltimore. He operated the little paper, which he called the *Afro-American*, in order to advertise his church and community enterprises. Reverend Alexander was "a better pastor than publisher,"[2] so he sold the paper to a Mr. John H. Murphy, Sr.

John Murphy was a man who earned his living by painting interiors. In that day people used a kind of paint called "whitewash" on their walls to make the rooms bright and clean. Murphy was the superintendent of the St. John AME Sunday School. He had been printing a small paper in his cellar to aid Maryland Sunday schools. With $200 borrowed from his wife Martha, he began to build what was to become a great newspaper chain!

He soon merged the original paper with another small paper; and, slowly, the *Afro-American* grew. At the age of fifty-two, Murphy decided to turn entirely to newspaper work and for twenty-five years he devoted himself to this work. When he died at the age of eighty-two in 1922, he left a successful publishing business to his sons, George, John, Daniel, Carl, and David.

MARTHA E. MURPHY   JOHN H. MURPHY, SR.

 May we let our light so shine that it will illuminate that which is good and beautiful, and magnify our Father which is in heaven. May we stand strong and firm against despair, falsehood, rudeness, hatred, pessimism and prejudice.—Carl Murphy, Editor-Publisher—1889-1967

It was Carl Murphy who became President of the Afro-American Company. This was the company that was to publish the *Afro-American* in Baltimore, Washington, Richmond, Newark, and Philadelphia. The Murphy family has had a great influence in the state of Maryland and in the nation. Generation after generation they excel in church and community activities, and in their publishing businesses.

In 1961 John H. Murphy, 3rd, grandson of the founder, took over from Dr. Carl Murphy. Today Mr. John J. Oliver, Sr. is the President of the *Afro-American* newspaper company. Mr. Ralph Matthews, Jr. is the Managing Editor. The newspaper today employs over 140 persons. In Baltimore, the *Afro-American* owns its buildings and printing plant. It is located at the intersection of Druid Hill Avenue and North Eutaw Street. Every week over 90,000 copies of the paper are sold. Each copy carries the words of Frederick Douglass: "We are Americans and as Americans we would speak to America."

Lillie May Jackson

Few Maryland people have contributed so single-mindedly as did Lillie Jackson to the cause of civil rights. For nearly 35 years she was

71

the head of the Maryland NAACP (1935-1970). She helped to build that organization from about a dozen members to an effective 20,000—member group by the time of her retirement in 1970.

Who could resist a woman who openly said, "A man must be honest, fair and decent." Who could stop a woman who used every legal means to obtain justice for all Maryland citizens?

Mrs. Jackson was born in Baltimore on May 25, 1889. Her parents were Charles Henry Carroll and Amanda Bowen Carroll. Lillie May Carroll attended public schools in Baltimore and graduated from high school in 1908.

She met and married young Keiffer Jackson and traveled about the country with him. The Jacksons showed movies to church groups, lectured and led a program of singing and prayer. After a time they decided to settle down in Baltimore City. Both Lillie and her husband worked hard to raise their four children and to provide education for them.

Lillie believed, and taught her children, that each person has a life's work to do. Further, to prepare for that work, each person must get the best education they can.

It was not until the late 1920s that Lillie became active in the civil rights movement. Remember, at that time few American blacks believed that civil rights for black Americans were obtainable. The incident that stirred Lillie Jackson to action was the refusal of Maryland colleges and universities to accept her two daughters who asked to enroll. Indignant, Mrs. Jackson began to work for black acceptance and made it her life's work to break down the racial barriers in Maryland. She faced years of work and many problems.

From 1931 on she became an important person in the civil rights movement in Maryland. She joined forces with Carl Murphy of the *Afro-American* newspaper chain. Her husband, Keiffer Jackson, supported her and her work in civil rights.

Mrs. Jackson fought her fight with spirit and dignity. She used American law to obtain social justice for black Marylanders. From 1935 to 1950 she and others brought law suits into the courts to open up the doors of higher education to black citizens. She and her allies won the battle by 1950.

A continuing legal fight by the Baltimore NAACP also opened up housing, pools, parks and improved employment practices for black Marylanders.

Honors flowed into the Jacksons' home. Lillie and her husband hosted many groups and individuals important to civil rights in America. For nearly sixty years the devoted couple shared their lives and hopes. After Mr. Jackson's death, Lillie Jackson went on with her

AFRO PRESIDENT John Murphy 3rd and Vice President Hubert H. Humphrey.

work and told young men and women in Maryland: "God helps those who help themselves. If you sit down on God, you'll just sit."

At her funeral in July, 1975, the Governor of Maryland spoke. Men and women of national prominence attended. Among the many professional people at the services were her four children and ten grandchildren---now attorneys, physicians, and businesspeople. Hundreds of humble citizens, too, drew close to the church to honor Lillie May Jackson who had cared about them. Mrs. Jackson had indeed done her life's work well.

Justice Thurgood Marshall

Thurgood Marshall was born in Baltimore, July 2, 1908. He attended public schools in Baltimore City. In 1930 he graduated with honors from Lincoln University, where he had gone intending to study dentistry. His interest changed to law, however, and in 1933 he graduated at the head of his class from Howard University Law School in Washington, D.C.

After graduation he practiced law in Baltimore and in 1934 became counsel for the Baltimore branch of the National Association for the Advancement of Colored People. In 1936 he joined the organization's national legal staff and, in 1938, he was appointed chief legal officer.

On September 4, 1929, he married Vivian Burey, who died in February 1955. In December, 1955, he married Cecilia A. Suyat. They have two children, Thurgood, Jr., and John William.

President Kennedy nominated Thurgood Marshall for appointment to the Second Circuit Court of Appeals in 1961 and the nomination was confirmed by the Senate. In the summer of 1965 President Johnson nominated Judge Marshall for appointment as Solicitor General of the United States. Judge Marshall took the oath of office in August of 1965.

President Lyndon Johnson nominated Judge Marshall in June of 1967 as an Associate Justice of the Supreme Court of the United States. Judge Marshall was confirmed by the Senate and took his oath of office on October 2, 1967. He is the first black American to become a Justice of the Supreme Court.

Justice Marshall has been awarded scores of national and local citations for his work in the field of civil rights.

1 **The Negro in Maryland Politics, 1870-1912,** by Maragaret Law Callcott, Johns Hopkins Press, Baltimore, Md., 1969.
2 **Good News For You!,** Afro American Company, Baltimore, Maryland, 1969.

... the great majority of black leaders felt that there was ... work to be done ... This was the use of political power—getting the ballot and putting it to proper use.

Benjamin Quarles

CHAPTER XI

YOUR VOTE

VOTING is such an important duty for every citizen that no story of Maryland would be complete without a brief outline of how one votes and a short history of the voting process.

Primary Elections

Before an official can be elected, he first (usually) must win the support of his own political party. Several people in one party may feel that they would like to run for the same office. These people make public appearances, talk to as many as they can, and try to persuade the registered voters of their party to support them in the Primary elections. But, when a person wins a Primary election, he still does not have the office he seeks. It only means that as far as his political party is concerned, he is its choice. Now he must face another round of speech making and appearances to try to get a majority of the registered voters to send him into office.

Voters are sometimes confused over the difference between primary and general elections. Voters may be annoyed, when during primary elections they find that they are not allowed to vote for a particular candidate because he is not registered as a member of the voter's political party! Voters should understand that primary elections are simply for selecting candidates from within a particular political party and that it is the general elections that then decide which person wins the office.

Registration

When a citizen wants to vote in an election, the first thing he must do is to go to the registration place for his area, or to the county or city court house. There, the voter's name and party are entered in large books, or "registers."

To register one must be a resident of Maryland, and of the county in which one resides (lives). The voter must have been a county resident for a certain amount of time, too. To vote one must be at least eighteen years of age.

Losing the Right to Vote

You may lose your right to vote if you have ever been convicted of certain serious crimes after becoming an adult. Also, a person whose mind is unsound may not vote. Elections laws, further, stop from voting those persons who have been found guilty of bribery in elections or of voting in an unfair manner (attempting to vote twice, for example).

Absentee Votes

Sometimes it is not possible for a citizen, even though properly registered, to be at his home voting place on election day. In that event, the law provides ways in which he can cast his vote by means of an "absentee ballot." People in the armed services do this, as do those other people who for some reason are away from home. If a voter is unable to leave home due to illness, that voter may still vote by using an absentee ballot which bears his doctor's signature.

General Elections

There are several kinds of general elections. We vote to help elect our national officials:—the President and Vice-President of the United States and members of the United States Congress. Congress is a name given to cover the two "houses," the House of Representatives, whose members are called Congressmen; and the Senate, whose members are called Senators.

Then, too, we vote to elect certain of our State officials:—the Governor, the Lieutenant-Governor, the Comptroller of the Treasury, and the Attorney General.

In addition to all of these, the voter in local elections casts his ballot in order to select representatives serving in the Maryland legislature, the General Assembly. These delegates may be elected to the State House of Delegates, or to serve in the State Senate. Usually, in the same election the voter also picks those who govern his county and the town or city in which he lives.

Public Opinion

Unfortunately, many citizens fail to register, and many registered voters fail to vote! It is a citizen's duty to study the candidates and to vote for those he believes will do the best job for his country, his state, his county or his town. A voter should not make the mistake of believing that his one vote is unimportant. The fact is that many elections have been decided by just one, or a very few, votes! One should, then, take an interest in politics, and inform himself so that he can vote intelligently at election time.

In the United States of America, we must never feel that "it's no use" to fight for what we believe is right. We have the power of free speech, the legal right to speak and vote, and the duty as citizens to see that capable, honest men and women are elected to office. It is a wonderful, a priceless heritage. Public opinion *is* important.

Even before coming to a voting age, young people should read newspapers and learn about their leaders in government. Then, when the time comes, they will be well prepared to speak out for their candidate and to cast a telling vote.

After reading this story of our state and our nation, we can have no doubt that our rights to rule ourselves and select our own leaders are important. Voting is a privilege that has been bought with the blood, tears, and years of devotion of our ancestors.

Your Maryland Heritage — Freedom

Americans are usually very jealous of their freedoms and rights. We engage in extended arguments over new laws, over taxation, over all manner of other public issues. In Maryland, we may have a right to be just a little extra proud of our freedoms. Here, many new ideas were first put into practice in the New World. Here there grew the belief that a person's individual life must be carefully safeguarded and his rights fully protected. The states bordering the Potomac River are known to historians as "the cradle of democracy." In Maryland and Virginia there were men, from the very first days of settlement, who believed in the sacredness of individual rights, dignity, and freedom—whatever the rank of the person or whatever amount of property he owned.

So used to the idea of each man having these rights are we, that it seems strange to discover that, when the colonies were first settled, the lower classes and poor people were thought of as inferior and possibly little more than slaves or serfs.

We have seen how much George Calvert, the First Lord Baltimore, believed in giving freedom of worship to all. His son Cecil, too, made sure that this freedom was given the settlers of Maryland.

Act of Religious Toleration

Complete freedom of worship was an idea that even Marylanders could not understand. Still, in 1649, they created a law that was far

77

A monument in St. Mary's County, a memorial to the establishment of the right to religious toleration in Maryland.

Maryland Dept. of Economic Development

ahead of its time. It was actually written by Cecil Calvert, though the first part may have been taken from his father, George Calvert's work. The Maryland Assembly called the law an "Act Concerning Religion," and it has come to be known as the "Toleration Act."

The Act said that "no person or persons whatsoever within this province . . . professing to believe in Jesus Christ, shall from henceforth be in any way troubled, molested, or discountenanced for or in respect of his or her religion, nor in the free exercise thereof . . ." The passage of such an act was a new and unusual thing for the early 1600's.[1]

Church and State Are Separate

As soon as the colony was settled, the second Lord Baltimore made sure that the church and the civil governments were entirely separate and required that the church authorities in Maryland obey this rule. He gave all religious groups in the colony great encouragement at the same time.

Puritans Upset Toleration Act

True, toleration in Maryland, just five years after the Toleration Act was passed, was temporarily suspended by the Puritans. But, if the Puritans did away with freedom of worship for a time, still they could "not erase its spirit from the minds of men." So it was that in 1661, when Cromwell had died and the English throne had been restored to King Charles II, Marylanders put the Act of Toleration back into force.

The Act then stayed in effect for thirty-one more years. Then, William and Mary, rulers of England, overruled the Act and required all English citizens to pay taxes to support the Anglican Church of England.

Still, though freedom of religion had its ups and downs in Maryland, we see that Maryland was among the first governments in the world to lead the way toward giving the people it governed the right to worship God as they chose.

Ordinary Men

In addition to freedom of religion in Maryland, another freedom was becoming evident in the same period of history. Men were beginning to feel that they had a right to govern themselves. The English government was so far away, and the Proprietors were usually living

In the United States House of Representatives, Congressman Parren J. Mitchell, 7th Congressional District of Maryland, has nine committees and subcommittees on which he acts.

His work with various groups in Maryland to improve urban areas and interracial relations is well known. He served as a commissioned officer in the U.S. Military. He has earned many awards for community service.

Parren Mitchell is a graduate of Morgan State University with a Master's Degree in Sociology, plus honorary degrees from the University of Maryland, Coppin State College and Morgan State University.

in England. Some sort of government on the spot appeared to be necessary. In all the English colonies in America there were such practices of self-government as town meetings and assemblies begun and demanded as a logical right.

In Maryland, while the men of wealth and rank were perhaps the primary leaders in the government of the colony, the freemen of lesser importance found that they could have a voice, too. In all of this the right to vote and the acceptance of the decision of the majority were important steps in the colonists' learning to govern themselves.

Maryland Voting Laws Change

Under the Maryland Constitution of 1776, which became the law of the land in November of that year, every free man in Maryland over twenty-one years of age, who owned at least fifty acres of land in the county in which he planned to live and vote, or property valued at forty pounds, and who had resided for one year of his residence in the county, had the right to vote. The law said further that those eligible and wishing to vote must go to the seat of government in each county, to vote *by voice* for his candidate!

The 1776 voting requirements, then, required that certain property be owned; and in those days no women were allowed to vote, and there was no secret ballot. All of the counties, by 1799, were divided into voting, or election, districts.

Property requirements to vote were partially removed in 1802 when most of the free, white, male citizens were given the right to vote. Also, in the years 1809 and 1810, voting was changed so that instead of voting by voice, written ballots were to be used. And, as already noted, in 1825 people of the Hebrew faith were given the right to vote.

Black men were enfranchised in 1870; that is, given the right to vote in elections in Maryland. However, fifty more years were to pass before the women of Maryland would be allowed to vote (1920). There is an exception to this last statement, however, in the way in which the town of Still Pond was incorporated.[2] When the town was incorporated by an act of the General Assembly in 1908, an important section of this act provided that the legal residents, women included, who were twenty-one years of age or over, and who had lived in the corporate limits of the town for at least six months, and who paid taxes, were to have the opportunity to vote for three commissioners. On Saturday, May 2, 1908, at least fourteen women were eligible to vote and three women did cast ballots, and so, according to a 1908 newspaper

Dr. Aris T. Allen, a member of the Maryland State Senate, was born in San Antonia, Texas. He attended elementary school there for a time but then his schooling was interrupted for some ten years. The young black man did not stop studying, however, during this time. He learned automobile mechanics, radio repair, carpentry, sheet metal work, pharmacy and drafting. By 1930 he was working during the day in Chicago, Illinois and attending high school in the evenings. In 1936 he moved to Washington, D.C. to work for the federal government and continued to study at night, at Dunbar High School, Howard University.

Senator Robert L. Douglass is the founder and President of the Baltimore Electronics Associates, an electronics manufacturing firm in Baltimore City. The drive that enabled him to establish this business in 1968 had brought him through years of university and graduate study, and service as an officer in the U.S. Army. Teaching, working as an electronics design engineer, and working in systems engineering, Mr. Douglass steadily learned the electronics design business.

In 1947 he married Bernice V. Sales. He and his wife have four children and two grandchildren.

Mr. Douglass became interested in politics and was elected to the City Council of Baltimore in 1967, serving there until elected to the Maryland State Senate in 1974. In the Senate Mr. Douglass strives to improve the laws of Maryland and to make them beneficial to all Maryland citizens.

He is active in programs to prevent drug abuse, to care for the ill, to assist black businessmen and businesswomen. He has worked for tax reform Bill, for community schools and for many public service organizations.

Delegate Walter R. Dean, Jr. was born in Baltimore City and graduated from Dunbar High School in 1953. After a four-year enlistment in the U.S. Air Force, Mr. Dean returned to college and graduated from Morgan State University in 1962. Still not satisfied that he was equipped to do the work he wished, he attended the Graduate School of Social Work at the University of Maryland, receiving a Master's Degree in Social Work in 1969.

For a time Mr. Dean worked as a reporter for the *Afro-American* newspapers. He is now an assistant professor in Urban Affairs at the Community College of Baltimore.

Delegate Dean is serving his third term as a member of the Maryland House of Delegates. He was first elected to the General Assembly in 1970.

81

account, "they became the first women in the State of Maryland to exercise the privilege of suffrage." However, with this exception, women in Maryland were not allowed to vote until 1920.

Many other changes in voting procedures have been put into practice, such as voting by machine, two-party poll-watching practices, redistricting of the State in order to give places with more population more representation, and other changes. Voting practices are still being altered, as, for example, the recent change in the voting age from a minimum age of twenty-one to that of eighteen.

In the State House

There are six black Senators and fourteen black Delegates in the Maryland General Assembly today. The Senators are: Dr. Aris T. Allen from Anne Arundel County; Senators Clarence W. Blount, Robert L. Douglass, Clarence M. Mitchell, III and Verda F. Welcome are from Baltimore City. Senator Tommie Broadwater is from Prince George's County.

The fourteen Delegates are: Troy Brailey; Joseph A. Chester, Sr.; Frank M. Conaway; Walter R. Dean, Jr.; Isaiah (Ike) Dixon, Jr.; John W. Douglass; Nathaniel Exum; Hattie N. Harrison; Lena K. Lee; Margaret H. Murphy; Wendell H. Phillips; Howard P. Rawlings; Sylvania R. Woods, Jr.; and Larry Young.

Delegate John W. Douglass was elected to the Maryland General Assembly in 1970. His specialty in the State House is in the field of finance. He is a member of the House of Delegates, House Appropriations Committee.

With action in the House of Delegates and by writing detailed studies, Delegate Douglass has done much to assist minorities in gaining employment opportunities. He has urged reforms in the pension laws of Baltimore City.

1 There were provisions in the Toleration Act for the severe punishment of the crime of blasphemy, that is, cursing or reviling God. Reading the Act today, too, you may wonder if perhaps Jewish people were treated badly. There were very few members of the Hebrew religion in the colony. Happily, the records show no persecution of Jewish families, though it was 1825 before they gained the right to vote.

2 This information was brought to the author's attention by Dr. William H. Wroten, Jr., Chairman of the Department of History and Political Science, of the Salisbury State College. The incorporation of Still Pond was accomplished via the introduction of House of Delegates Bill #21-1/2 by the Kent County delegates, on February 20, 1980. The Bill was accepted on March 20 of that same year. The Bill became law (Chapter 160, pages 893-901) with final approval as law on March 30, 1908.

I am somebody! Excel! Excel! Excel!
Rev. Jesse Jackson in his Push for Excellence program.

CHAPTER XII

MEN AND WOMEN OF MARYLAND TODAY

What shall I do with my life? Every boy and girl asks this question. Do you have to earn fame and wealth to live a happy and successful life? The answer to that is, "Of course not!" A happy and successful life may come to us from satisfying, interesting work. It may be that the adventure of being a father or a mother will bring us content as we see our children grow around us. The respect and approval of your family and friends make you happy. It is enjoyable to learn, to work, and to relax with singing and sports. Friendship is an important part of a rich, full life.

Is a rich and famous actor more successful than a man who is a loved father, and who has worked for his family for many years? Is a popular ballerina more successful than a woman who has worked hard and made a home for her family?

As Americans we are free to try many things, learn many skills, attempt many kinds of work until we find one that we enjoy. Each of us, even if we never get mentioned in textbooks, are needed to help develop our state, our Maryland.

Maryland has given the world many interesting people. Some of them are described here. Each of these found work that interested them.

Tamara Dobson

"Tall is beautiful." her mother insisted. Young Tamara Dobson struggled with this thought as she puzzled over her problem of being one of the tallest students in her class at Harriet Beecher Stowe Elementary School. It took will power to refuse to slump or wear flat shoes in an effort to look shorter. Instead, Tamara held her head gracefully high, her shoulders square, her back regally straight.

Her entire family is tall, her father, her mother, her two brothers and a sister. As she grew up in Baltimore, Maryland, Tamara soaked up her studies in public schools, preparing herself for an exciting life. What was that to be? She didn't know then, but she had high hopes.

While studying and growing, Tamara helped in the beauty salon her mother operates in West Baltimore on Liberty Heights and Dennison Street. She worked her way up from shampoo girl to

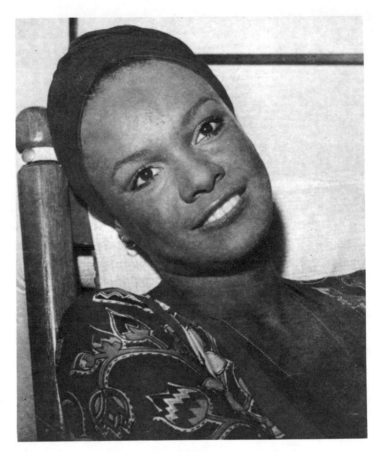

Tamara Dobson

manicurist to licensed beautician. This gave Tamara independence. She could always earn her living proudly with her trade.

After graduation from Western High School, Tamara became interested in fashion illustration. She enrolled in the Maryland Institute of Art to learn this skill. While there, a representative from Hutzler's Department Store came to talk with the art students about fashion, design, and marketing fashion. He met young Tamara and said, "You should be in New York, working as a model. You have poise." The gentleman sent her to Bill Blass the well-known dress designer in New York. Blass sent her to a top model agency. Her height seemed to be a point against her, yet her poise and beauty won her more and more modeling assignments. In 1969, her first year in New York, she became the darling of top photographers. In six months she earned $25,000 and spent most of it on her family.

Tamara Dobson is proud of her family. Her father works for the Pennsylvania Railroad and has over the years provided not only money but strength and guidance for his family. Tamara Dobson's mother, too, has worked long and hard for her family in her beauty salon. What Miss Dobson most appreciates about her mother she says is, "The behavior she taught me as a young person, how to talk to people, how to be polite, how to generate kindness instead of hate. My mother has style."

It was Sidney Poitier, a leading black actor, who suggested an acting career to Tamara Dobson when he met her in New York. Again, Miss Dobson did not simply "want" a career, but set to work preparing herself for it. She enrolled in ballet classes, took voice, fencing lessons and worked with a drama coach. When her opportunity came, she wanted to be ready for it.

"I studied for three years," she said, "working to pay for my lessons." She then came to Los Angeles for a vacation and was introduced to an agent. She was selected to play Yul Brynner's partner in a movie. After this short part was finished, Miss Dobson knew that she loved acting. Fortunately, Warner Brothers needed a black actress to star in a movie to be called *Cleopatra Jones*. Some 2500 girls were interviewed but Tamara Dobson was chosen for her star quality.

Today Tamara Dobson is an established actress and continues to study for more acting roles. The mind and body that she has trained all her life now help her withstand the stresses and demands of her career. Tamara Dobson, of Baltimore, Maryland, continues to grow.

James A. Porter

When James A. Porter was born in Baltimore in 1903, no one could guess that he would grow up to be a famous art historian and painter. True, he did learn to draw at an early age and loved pictures. By the time he had completed high school it was easy to see that he was bound to be an artist and a scholar.

Porter studied at Howard University; the Art Students League, in New York; at the Sorbonne in Paris, and finally completed his studies with a Master's Degree at the New York University. Through the years Porter not only painted and studied but traveled widely to see the art of the world.

Since 1946 he has held ten one-man shows. He is the author of the popular and scholarly, *Modern Negro Art* published in 1943, and of many articles on art.

James Porter was sent as a delegate to many conferences in this country and in Africa. In 1965, as art historian and painter, Porter was recognized at the National Gallery of Art's 25th anniversary as one of America's most outstanding men of the arts.

The writer of books on modern day art, Elton Fax, was born in Baltimore City in 1909. He is one of America's finest artists and illustrators. Both his writing and his drawings have brought out a proud interest in the American black citizen and in an African heritage.

By 1931, Fax had earned his Bachelor's Degree in Fine Arts from Syracuse University. For a time in the 1930s, he taught at Claflin University and at the Harlem Community Art Center. His work has been exhibited in many leading museums including the Baltimore Art Museum.

His most recent book is a series of articles and illustration, *Through Black Eyes*, which tells of his recent trips to Africa.

Clifton R. Wharton

Born in Baltimore at the turn of the century, Clifton R. Wharton went to Massachusetts as a young man to attend Boston University. There he earned his L.L.B. and LL.M. degrees in law.

In 1924 young Wharton became a law clerk at the United States State Department at an annual salary of $1,860. Steadily, faithfully, he continued to work and to learn.

Wharton became a man of reputation in the State Department. He became the nation's first black career minister when President Eisenhower appointed him Minister to Rumania in 1958. (The word "minister," in diplomatic circles, means a high United States official representative to a country.) Later, in 1961, Clifton Wharton became the first black American to be chosen as an envoy to a key European country when President Kennedy selected him to serve as Ambassador to Norway.

An article in the *Washington Post* newspaper, June 29, 1975, describes Mr. Wharton as "now retired, and basking in the success of his three sons, all Harvard graduates."

Note: "Ambassador's Fete," *Washington Post*, June 29, 1975, p. E12.

N. Louise Young, M.D.

Following her father's interest in medicine, N. Louise Young of Baltimore decided on an unusual career for a young black woman. She wanted to become a doctor.

Her father, Dr. Howard Young, had been a trailblazer himself, being the first black pharmacist in Maryland. Until 1945, the year of his death, he ran Young's Pharmacy. He backed his daughter in her desire to enter medicine. Louise Young received more encouragement from her mother, Estelle, who was a college graduate and a former teacher.

In fact, the reputation of her entire family must have encouraged Louise Young. After all, her grandfather was the Reverend Alfred Young, pastor of the Sharpe Street Methodist Episcopal Church in Baltimore. It is one of the oldest congregations serving black Baltimoreans and dates back to 1802.

With her heart set on becoming a doctor, Louise Young worked hard to do well in undergraduate school in the 1920s. She then entered the Howard University Medical School. Often she found that she was the only woman in the classroom. The hours of study and self discipline that medical school required were rewarded upon her graduation in 1930.

Now she must serve an internship at Freedman's Hospital. She served this demanding apprenticeship which all doctors undergo. She then went on to a residency at Providence Hospital, specializing in the care of women and problems relating to childbirth, that is, in gynecology and obstetrics. She was now Maryland's first black woman doctor.

She next accepted a position as staff physician for the Maryland Training School for Girls. Dr. Young served there from 1933 to 1940. During this time she also served as women's physician to Morgan State College (1935 to 1940). Not only had Dr. Young realized her dream of becoming a physician, but she became an outstanding Maryland doctor. She has headed several hospital departments of obstetrics and has served on many committees.

While pursuing her medical career, Louise Young met and married a Marylander, Dr. Gilbert Caldwell, a dentist. Some time following his death, Louise Young married again, becoming Mrs. William E. Spenser in private life.

When not serving on her many boards or working as a physician, Dr. Young takes time to enjoy the out-of-doors, to ride horseback and to do modeling. Dr. Young is a woman who has not neglected her private and family life in search of a career, yet has won acclaim as an outstanding doctor and for her service to her city and state.

Sugar Ray Leonard, Olympic boxing champion, 1976. With him, his son Little Ray.

Craig Herndon photograph, The Washington Post.

Sugar Ray Leonard

While still a boy, Sugar Ray Leonard moved to Palmer Park, Maryland, with his family. This was to make a great difference in his life. Near his new home he discovered the Palmer Park Recreation Center. Soon the activities of the boxing club there became an important part of his week. He knew that he must not only train his body, but also his mind, in order to excel at boxing. From his classes in the local high school, he tried to learn as much as he could as a part of his preparation.

In the recreation center there was the Frank P. Rubini Boxing Club and training youngsters in boxing was volunteer coach Dave Jacobs. Jacobs, in 1974 was named "coach of the year," by the Amateur Athletic Union. Coach Jacobs saw young Leonard's unusual determination and coached the young man skillfully. "All the way," Leonard now says, "Jake has been at my side, he's been like a father to me."

Sugar Ray dared to dream of winning the top amateur boxing prize, the Olympic gold medal. It seemed unlikely, yet for five years Sugar Ray persisted, "I kept on, keeping on!"

Each morning at 5:30 a.m. he climbed out of bed to run for miles, toughening and training his body. Under Jacob's care, Leonard became wise in boxing moves, in planning his bouts. The qualifications came and went and Leonard's efforts paid off. He was selected to go to the Olympic Games in Montreal.

For two months in Montreal, in the Olympic Games of 1976, Leonard kept up his training pace. When the Games ended, it was Sugar Ray Leonard, a Maryland man, who held the gold medal in his hand. He was recognized as the best amateur boxer in his class in the world.

Leonard does not intend to continue in boxing, rather he plans to go to college to obtain the degree that will help him train others in physical education, to coach new boxers. Leonard hopes to work in his Maryland hometown and encourage other young athletes, as his coach encouraged him---all the way to the Olympic gold medal.

And Many More

The persons mentioned here are only a sampling of the many citizens of Maryland that we can point to with pride. Other names that come to mind are: Milton B. Allen, Eubie Blake, Lucille Clifton, Clarence Mitchell, Juanita Jackson Mitchell, Dr. Benjamin Quarles, and many others.

A Second Reconstruction

In his very complete book on the Civil Rights Movement from 1940 to 1970, *Walls Come Tumbling Down*, author Thomas R. Brooks notes a "second reconstruction." He sees from various census and other federal reports, that membership in unions is up, that better housing is now available for blacks, and that more black Americans are going to college than ever before. Interestingly enough, these students are enrolled, for the most part, in desegregated colleges and universities.

Job opportunities, too, according to Dr. Brooks, are opening up not just in cities, nor in the North, but in rural areas and in the South.

Dr. Brooks gives us many statistical proofs that all Americans are moving rapidly toward mutual understanding as we live and work together.

You are magic.

Anonymous

1980 POPULATION STATISTICS

Taken from *The Statistical Abstract of the United States, 1982-1983*, U. S. Department of Commerce, Bureau of the Census, Washington, D.C.

Table 38, "Black Population by Age --- By State: 1980

MARYLAND

Under 5 years of age	77,000
5 - 14	180,000
15-24	207,000
24-44	289,000
45-64	149,000
65 and over	58,000
Total Black Population of Maryland	960,000
Total Population of Maryland (All)	4,300,000

[Through **1960**, as of **April 1.** 1940 based on complete count; 1950, on 20-percent sample; and 1960, on 25-percent sample. Beginning **1970**, as of **March,** based on Current Population Survey; see text, p. 2. Excludes Armed Forces, except members living off post or with families on post. Beginning **1980**, excludes inmates of institutions]

AGE AND YEAR	ALL PERSONS					BLACK PERSONS				
	Percent not high school graduates		Percent with 4 years of high school or more		Median school years completed [1]	Percent not high school graduates		Percent with 4 years of high school or more		Median school years completed [1]
	Total	With less than 5 yrs. of school	Total	College, 4 yrs. or more		Total	With less than 5 yrs. of school	Total	College, 4 yrs. or more	
25 years and over:										
1940	75.5	13.7	24.5	4.6	8.6	92.7	42.0	7.3	1.3	5.7
1950	65.7	11.1	34.3	6.2	9.3	87.1	32.9	12.9	2.1	6.8
1960	58.9	8.3	41.1	7.7	10.6	79.9	23.8	20.1	3.1	8.0
1970	44.8	5.3	55.2	11.0	12.2	66.3	15.1	33.7	4.5	9.9
1980 [2]	31.4	3.4	68.6	17.0	12.5	48.8	9.2	51.2	7.9	12.0
1981	30.3	3.3	69.7	17.1	12.5	47.1	7.9	52.9	8.2	12.1
25–29 years:										
1940	61.9	5.9	38.1	5.9	10.3	(NA)	27.7	11.6	1.6	7.0
1950	49.5	4.7	52.8	7.7	12.0	80.4	16.8	22.2	2.7	8.6
1960	39.2	2.8	60.7	11.1	12.3	62.3	7.0	37.7	4.8	9.9
1970	24.6	1.1	75.4	16.4	12.6	43.9	2.5	56.2	7.3	12.2
1980 [2]	14.6	.8	85.4	22.5	12.9	23.4	.6	76.6	11.5	12.6
1981	13.7	.7	86.3	21.3	12.8	22.7	.5	77.3	11.5	12.6

NA Not available.   [1] For definition of median, see Guide to Tabular Presentation.   [2] Population controls based on the 1980 census; see text, p. 2.

[**Persons 25 years old and over.** Persons of Spanish origin may be of any race. For definition of median, see Guide to Tabular Presentation. See headnote, table 225. See also *Historical Statistics, Colonial Times to 1970,* series H 602–617]

YEAR, RACE, AND SEX	Population (1,000)	PERCENT OF POPULATION COMPLETING—							Median school years completed
		Elementary school			High school		College		
		0–4 years	5–7 years	8 years	1–3 years	4 years	1–3 years	4 years or more	
1960, all races	**99,438**	**8.3**	**13.8**	**17.5**	**19.2**	**24.6**	**8.8**	**7.7**	**10.6**
White	89,581	6.7	12.8	18.1	19.3	25.8	9.3	8.1	10.9
Male	43,259	7.4	13.7	18.7	18.9	22.2	9.1	10.3	10.7
Female	46,322	6.0	11.9	17.8	19.6	29.2	9.5	6.0	11.2
Black	9,054	23.8	24.2	12.9	19.0	12.9	4.1	3.1	8.0
Male	4,240	28.3	23.9	12.3	17.3	11.3	4.1	2.8	7.7
Female	4,814	19.8	24.5	13.4	20.5	14.3	4.1	3.3	8.6
1970, all races	**109,310**	**5.3**	**9.1**	**13.4**	**17.1**	**34.0**	**10.2**	**11.0**	**12.2**
White	98,112	4.2	8.3	13.6	16.5	35.2	10.7	11.6	12.2
Male	46,606	4.5	8.8	13.9	15.6	30.9	11.3	15.0	12.2
Female	51,506	3.9	7.8	13.4	17.3	39.0	10.1	8.6	12.2
Black	10,089	15.1	16.7	11.2	23.3	23.4	6.9	4.5	9.9
Male	4,619	18.6	16.0	11.1	21.9	22.2	6.7	4.6	9.6
Female	5,470	12.1	17.3	11.3	24.5	24.4	6.0	4.4	10.2
1980, all races [1]	**130,409**	**3.4**	**6.0**	**8.2**	**13.9**	**36.8**	**14.9**	**17.0**	**12.5**
White	114,763	2.6	5.4	8.3	13.1	37.6	15.1	17.8	12.5
Male	54,389	2.7	5.5	8.3	12.5	33.1	15.8	22.1	12.6
Female	60,374	2.5	5.3	8.4	13.7	41.6	14.5	14.0	12.5
Black	12,927	9.2	11.1	7.2	21.3	30.8	12.5	7.9	12.0
Male	5,717	11.4	10.6	7.1	19.9	29.8	13.5	7.7	12.0
Female	7,209	7.4	11.5	7.4	22.4	31.5	11.7	8.1	12.0
Spanish origin	5,934	15.8	16.0	8.7	14.9	26.7	10.2	7.7	10.7
Male	2,825	16.5	15.4	8.5	14.8	24.0	11.8	9.2	10.9
Female	3,109	15.3	16.7	8.9	15.0	29.2	8.7	6.2	10.6
1981, all races	**132,899**	**3.3**	**5.8**	**7.7**	**13.6**	**37.6**	**15.1**	**17.1**	**12.5**
White	116,647	2.6	5.1	7.9	12.8	38.5	15.3	17.8	12.6
Male	55,213	2.7	5.3	7.7	12.3	34.1	15.7	22.2	12.6
Female	61,435	2.5	5.0	8.1	13.3	42.4	14.9	13.8	12.5
Black	13,259	7.9	11.1	6.8	21.4	31.6	13.1	8.2	12.1
Male	5,848	9.3	10.2	7.1	20.1	31.1	13.9	8.2	12.1
Female	7,411	6.8	11.8	6.5	22.4	32.1	12.4	8.2	12.1
Spanish origin	6,308	15.6	16.7	8.8	14.4	26.3	10.5	7.7	10.7
Male	2,993	15.2	16.5	9.0	13.9	24.5	11.3	9.7	11.0
Female	3,316	16.1	16.8	8.7	14.9	27.9	9.8	5.9	10.5

[1] Population controls based on the 1980 census; see text p. 2.

Source of tables 225 and 226: U.S. Bureau of the Census, *U.S. Census of Population: 1960,* vol. I, and *Current Population Reports,* series P–20, No. 207, and unpublished data.

Courtesy U. S. Department of Commerce, Bureau of the Census, Washington, D.C. *The Statistical Abstract of the United States, 1982-1983. p. 143.*

John Pardlow daily takes hundreds of people and this Metro bus, worth over $50,000, safely over many miles of suburban roadways. He must be a good driver, polite, patient and able to handle emergencies.

Author photograph.

John King, media consultant, is training for his Commercial Pilot's certificate. He is talking with an instructor at Freeway Airport, Mitchellville, Maryland.

Author photograph.

Photograph courtesy MCPB.

Studio Supervisor, Dwight Pearman, at work at the Maryland Center for Public Broadcasting.

Some members of the Maryland State Senate.

Taken from *The Maryland Manual, 1981-1982*.

CLARENCE W. BLOUNT, Democrat, District 41. Born in Beaufort County, N.C. Attended Baltimore City public schools; Morgan State University, B.A., 1950; The Johns Hopkins University, M.L.A., 1965; Georgetown University. Educator. Served in World War II; awarded Combat Commission. Assistant Senate Majority Leader. Chairman, Health and Education Subcommittee. Vice-chairman, Budget and Taxation Committee. Member, Executive Nominations Committee; Plain Language Study Committee; Capital Projects; Governor's Commission on Law Enforcement and the Administration of Justice; Executive Board and National Steering Committee, Education Commission of the States; Southern Regional Education Board. Member, National Democratic Committee. Member, Academy of Political Science; Academy of Political and Social Science; Morgan State University Alumni Association; The Johns Hopkins University Alumni Association; Baltimore Urban League; NAACP; Alpha Phi Alpha Fraternity. Member, Board of Trustees, Provident and Sinai Hospitals; Western Maryland College. Member, Advisory Board, United Student Aid. Member, Advisory Council, National Association of Community and Junior Colleges; National Educational Forum; Urban Affairs Committee, N.C.S.L.; Advanced Leadership Program Services, Mid-Atlantic Region. Chairman, Urban Services Commission, Baltimore City. Member, League of Handicapped and Crippled Children. Received numerous distinguished service awards. Married. Member of the Senate since 1971. Member, Legislative Policy Committee. District office: 4811 Liberty Heights Ave., Baltimore 21207; tel. 466-1197. Annapolis office: 100 James Bldg., 21401; tel. 841-3697.

TOMMIE BROADWATER, JR., Democrat, District 25. Born in Washington, D.C., June 9, 1942. Attended Prince George's County public schools; Southeastern University. Bail bondsman and businessman. Member, Prince George's County Democratic State Central Committee, 1970–1974; Glenarden Town Council, 1968–1973. Member, Maryland Blue Law Commission, 1974. Member, Ploughman and Fisherman Democratic Club; NAACP; Prince George's Chamber of Commerce; D.C. Chamber of Commerce; Boys and Girls Club of Glenarden; Y.M.C.A.; Bondsmen's Association; P.T.A. Married. Member of the Senate since 1975. District office: 5611 Landover Road, Hyattsville 20784; tel. 277-7500. Annapolis office: 215 James Bldg., 21401; tel. 841-3148.

CLARENCE M. MITCHELL III, Democrat, District 38. Born in St. Paul, Minn., December 14, 1939. Attended Baltimore public schools; Gonzaga High School, Washington, D.C.; University of Maryland; Morgan State University; University of Baltimore Law School. Mortgage banker, real estate broker, and consultant. Former member, Young Democrats of Maryland; Baltimore Junior Chamber of Commerce. Member, Y.M.C.A.; NAACP; Kappa Alpha Psi; Urban League; Prince Hall Masons; and other civic and fraternal organizations. Two children, Clarence Mitchell IV and Lisa Mitchell. Recipient of many awards for outstanding leadership and citizenship from government, private industry, and community groups. Member of the House of Delegates, 1963–1967. Member of the Senate since 1967 (Deputy Majority Leader, 1975–1978; Majority Whip, 1979). President, National Black Caucus of State Legislators, 1979–1981. District office: 1239 Druid Hill Ave., Baltimore 21217; tel. 523-4222. Annapolis office: 306 James Bldg., 21401; tel. 841-3612.

VERDA F. WELCOME, Democrat, District 40. Born in Lake Lure, N.C. Attended North Carolina and Delaware public schools; Coppin Normal School; Morgan State College, B.S., 1939; New York University, M.S., 1943; Columbia University. Former teacher. Public member, State Department Foreign Service Selection Boards. Member, Americans for Democratic Action; Board of Governors, 4th District Democratic Organization of Baltimore City, Inc.; Valiant Women's Democratic Club; Baltimore Urban League. Board member, Citizen's Planning and Housing Association; League of Women Voters; Maryland State Division, American Association of University Women. Life member, NAACP. Member, National Order of Women Legislators; Advisory Board, Provident Hospital. Founder and member, Mondawmin Improvement Association. Life member, Delta Sigma Theta Sorority. Received many distinguished service awards and citations. Married. Member of the House of Delegates, 1959–1963. Member of the Senate since 1963. Vice-chairman, Executive Nominations Committee. Member, Senate Finance Committee. District office: 3423 Holmes Avenue, Baltimore 21217; tel. 669-7110. Annapolis office: 101 Pres. Wing, James Bldg., 21401; tel. 841-3673.

Maryland State House, Annapolis, Md.
Photograph courtesy Office of Tourist Dev., Md Dept. of ECD.

It is not all training and work in the U.S. Navy. There are times for sports and relaxation, too.

Photographs courtesy Naval Air Station, Patuxent River, Md.

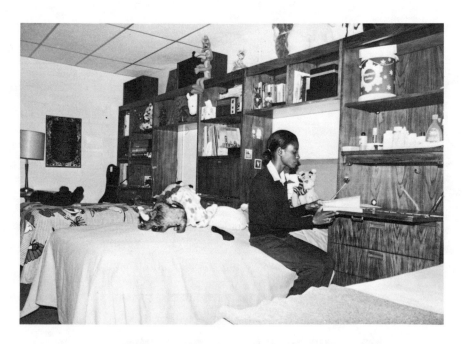

YNSN Rose Cooper relaxes in her room in the enlisted quarters for single personnel.

Photo courtesy NAS Patuxent River, Md.

96

Charles Center, Baltimore City. Workers from offices take a break.

Md Div of Tourism photo by Bob Willis.

Both farming and fishing are important in Maryland. Many people work on the land, while others like to work on the water. Both occupations help make Maryland the "Land of Pleasant Living."

Author photograph.

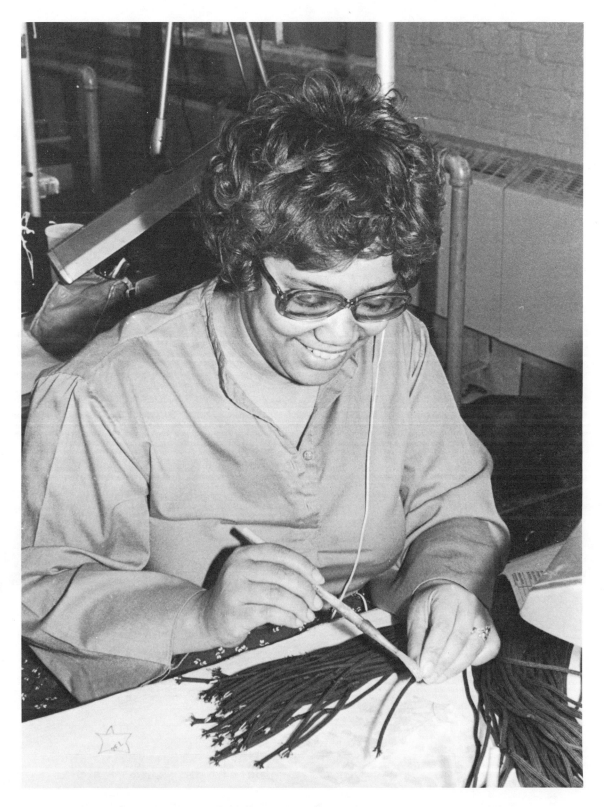

**In Maryland, thousands of people work   making
electrical and electronic equipment.**

Photo courtesy the Western Electric Company.

This man is showing a fellow worker how to shape metal. These workers are part of the skilled Maryland work force.

Photo courtesy the Western Electric Co.

The luxury Liner, *S.S. Nieuw Amsterdam,* of Holland America Cruises, leaves the Port of Baltimore.

Photo courtesy the Div. of Tourist Dev. Md Dept. ECD.

Graphic artist, Reginal Blackstone, is busy with a design at the Maryland Center for Public Broadcasting, Owings Mills, Md.

**Many people work
in Maryland's
building trades.**

Author photograph.

...others work on ships!

Md Office of Tourist Development,MDECD.

Dependable Service
Regardless of Weather Conditions
the Trains Go Through!
Baltimore and Ohio Railroad

Transportation is a very important occupation in Maryland. The state has railways, waterways, airports and miles of fine highways.

Photo courtesy Md. Div. of Tourist Development, MDECD.

Some people work in shops.

Author photograph.

**Law enforcement officers
at work in
Prince George's County.**
Author photograph.

**Annapolis is such a beautiful town that it attracts many
tourists. Tourism is an important part of the Maryland
economy.**

Author Photograph.

BIBLIOGRAPHY

Andrews, Matthew Page, *History of Maryland, Province and State*, reprint of 1929 edition, Hatboro, Penna.: Tradition Press, 1965.

Angell, Pauline K., *To the Top of the World*, Chicago, New York, San Francisco: Rand McNally & Company, 1964.

Bedini, Silvio A., *The Life of Benjamin Banneker*, New York: Charles Scribner's Sons, 1972.

Bergman, Peter M., *The Chronological History of the Negro in America*, New York: Harper & Row, 1968.

Brooks, Thomas R., *Walls Come Tumbling Down: A History of the Civil Rights Movement, 1940-1970*. Englewood Cliffs, N.J.: Prentice-Hall, Inc., 1974.

Burchard, Peter, *One Gallant Rush*, New York: St. Martin's Press, 1965.

Burke, Joan Martin, *Civil Rights*, 2d ed., New York: R. R. Bowker Co., 1974.

Callcott, Margaret Law, *The Negro in Maryland Politics, 1870-1912*, Baltimore: Johns Hopkins Press, 1969.

Conrad, Earl, *Harriett Tubman*, Washington: The Associated Publishers, 1943.

Foner, Philip S., *Life and Writings of Frederick Douglass*, in four volumes, New York: International Publishers, 1950.

Fraenkel, Osmond K., *The Rights We Have*, 2d ed., revised. New York: Thomas Y. Crowell Co., 1974.

Graham, Shirley, *Your Most Humble Servant*, New York: Julian Messner, 1949, 1967.

Greenbie, Sydney and Marjorie Barstow Greenbie, *Anna Ella Carroll and Abraham Lincoln*, Tampa: University of Tampa Press with Falmouth Publishing House, Inc., 1952.

Helmes, Winifred G., ed., *Notable Maryland Women*. Cambridge, Md.: Tidewater Publishers, 1977.

Herring, Hubert, with Helen B., *A History of Latin America*, Chapter 4, "The African Background," New York: Alfred A. Knopf, 1955, 3d Ed., 1969.

Hughes, Langston and Milton Meltzer, *A Pictorial History of the Negro in America*, 3rd Edition Revised, New York: Crown Publishers, Inc., 1968.

Miller, Floyd, *Ahdoolo!* A Biography of Matthew A. Henson, New York: E. P. Dutton & Company, Inc., 1963.

Morsbach, Mabel, *The Negro in American Life*, New York: Harcourt, Brace & World, Inc., 1966, 1967.

Murphy, E. Jefferson, *Understanding Africa*, New York: Thomas Y. Crowell Company, 1969.

Oliver, Roland and J. D. Fage, *A Short History of Africa*, New York: New York University Press, 1963.

Parkes, Henry Bamford, *The United States of America, A History*, New York: Alfred Knopf, 1959.

Ploski, Harry A., compiler, ed., *The Afro American: The Negro Almanac*, New York: Bellwether Co., 1976.

Pogue, Robert E. T., *Yesterday in Old St. Mary's County*, New York: Hearthstone Press, 1968.

Quarles, Benjamin, *Black Abolitionists*, New York: Oxford University Press, 1969.

Quarles, Benjamin, *Frederick Douglass*, Washington: The Associated Publishers, Inc., 1948.

Quarles, Benjamin, *The Negro in the Making of America*, New York: McMillan Company, 1969. London: Collier-McMillan, Ltd., 1969.

Redding, Jay Saunders, *The Negro*, Washington: Potomac Books, Inc., 1967.

Rose, Arnold, *The Negro in America*, New York: Harper and Brothers, 1944, 1948.

Scharf, J. Thomas, *History of Maryland*, three volumes, reprint of 1879 edition. Hatboro, Penna.: Tradition Press, 1967.

Schaun, George and Virginia, *The Story of Early Maryland*, Annapolis: Greenberry Publications, 1968.

Stampp, Kenneth M., *The Peculiar Institution*, Slavery in the Ante-Bellum South, New York: Alfred A. Knopf, Inc., 1956.

Wagandt, Charles L., *The Mighty Revolution, Negro Emancipation in Maryland, 1862-1864*, Baltimore: Johns Hopkins Press, 1964.

Weems, John Edward, *Peary, the Explorer and the Man*, Boston: Houghton Mifflin Company, 1967.

Col. George M. Brooks, Director, Maryland Civil Defense and Disaster Preparedness Agency.
Photorgaph courtesy MCDDPA

Michael A. Tomlinson, Meteorologist, appears on programs produced at the Maryland Center for Public Broadcasting, Owings Mills, and transmitted to some 200 stations coast to coast.
Photograph courtesy Maryland Center for Public Broadcasting

107

INDEX

Everett L. Marshburn, executive producer, public affairs, Maryland Center for Public Broadcasting.
courtesy MCPB

Cherryale Burge, an associate TV producer, MCPB.
Courtesy MCPB